Better Homes and Gardens®

easy
greeting cards

Favorites from the Editors
of SCRAPBOOKS ETC®

Better Homes and Gardens®

EASY greeting CARDS

Favorites from the Editors of SCRAPBOOKS ETC.®

WILEY

John Wiley & Sons, Inc.

contents

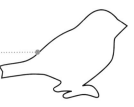

enjoy!

In the daily flurry of e-mails, texts, and social media exchanges, the act of receiving a real, physical note is something to welcome. Make it a handmade greeting, and the message becomes even more special, perhaps even something to cherish for a long time.

But, you ask, why make a card when you can just make a quick trip to the store to buy one? For crafters, there's enjoyment in creating a handmade card filled with heart— not only because of the sentiment written inside, but because of the care that was taken in making it. Papers and embellishments are chosen with care, and messages can be tailored to the recipient's personality. Instead of just a flat, printed one-size-fits-all card plucked from the sea of greeting cards at the big box store, a handmade message brims with texture, dimension, color, and personal elements. A handmade card is truly an expression that shows you care.

Just because you've decided to make a handmade card, it doesn't mean you have to spend all day making it or agonizing over the process. That's where this book comes in. Inside, you'll find a collection of over 250 cards for all kinds of occasions throughout the year, all with simple yet clever designs that will appeal to everyone. From birthday, thank-you, get-well, congrats, and just-because cards, to holiday greetings, party invitations, cards for newlyweds, and even wedding save-the-date cards, you'll find something to fit every card-giving need.

Not only will you be inspired by the selection, you'll learn some new techniques, too. As you browse through the pages, keep an eye out for bonus instructions for techniques that every card maker should have in their skill set. Learn how to paper-piece, how to apply a rub-on transfer, how to heat emboss, and even how to make your own letterpress cards. In all, there are over 15 step-by-step techniques you can learn that will give your cards a more polished look.

As you make your cards, our hope is that you relish not only the act of giving the card, but the process of making one, too.

birthdays

Wish someone special another happy year with fun
and colorful birthday greetings—or choose a one-of-a-kind invitation
to bring friends and family together for the big celebration.

another year wiser!

"Who" is having a birthday? Open up this owl to find out all the party details. The bird shape is easy to re-create by starting with a rectangle and scooping out the top with scissors to make two pointed ears. Scallop-style patterned paper makes a wise choice to create a featherlike body, while punched and layered circles are an easy way to make those signature big eyes. DESIGN: LISA STORMS

another year
wiser!

make a wish

Need a card in a hurry? Trim a trio of horizontal strips from patterned paper, round the corners, and layer them on the front of a card. Top it off with a tag frame and a mishmash of word stickers for the ultimate in quick-crafting.

DESIGN: AMY LICHT

happy birthday

Topped with a sparkly crown, this stylized bird is here to wish someone a happy birthday. Simple chipboard shapes including circles and petals create the basic form of the bird, which is embellished with small cardstock piecings and a heart brad to finish it off. The blades of grass are trimmed from white cardstock, then smeared with green ink pads to create the irregular shading.

DESIGN: CATHY BLACKSTONE

happy 32 years

Play up a game-night party theme with this fun-loving invitation using playing cards. Pick out the numbers needed to create the birthday age, then adhere them in a fanned-out fashion to the front of a patterned paper card base. Print out a greeting and punch it into a circle and attach it just below a colorful ribbon wrapped around the cards. DESIGN: LISA STORMS

beth's birthday bash

Prepare for a big birthday blowout with this party invitation that's sure to catch your guests' attention. It's easy to make multiples using a skinny folded cardstock rectangle for the base, adding a crimped cardstock layer to the front, and adding patterned paper flames between the layers at the top. Colorful cardstock strips printed with the party info add a bit of color to the front of the invite. DESIGN: LISA STORMS

Don't spill
the beans!

You're invited to a
Surprise Party
for Janet's 30th birthday!

riday, March 18th @ 7 p
stonehi clubhouse

shhh...

This little box is actually
a birthday party invite in
disguise! Take off the top to
reveal the message inside—
an invitation to a top-secret,
surprise birthday party. Print
the message on cardstock
and glue it to the inside of
the box, then add loose jelly
beans for a fun and colorful
addition that serves as a
reminder to not "spill the
beans." DESIGN: LISA STORMS

birthday blast

Space lovers will think this rocket-themed card is simply out of this world. Use the patterns on *page 180* to cut out the pieces from cardstock, keeping in mind which parts you'll be glittering. For consistent glitter, apply an adhesive sheet to your cardstock, and wait to remove the liner until it's time to add the glitter. Give your rocket a passenger with a robot-shaped brad attached to the window. DESIGN: CATHY BLACKSTONE

Hope your birthday is a BLAST!

put on your Party Hat and...

CELEBRATE!!

put on your party hat

Tissue paper scraps burst with color and texture at the top and bottom of this hat. Attach the party hat on a circle background and layer it on a contrasting pink-edged circle for extra interest. Hand write your birthday message onto a strip of white paper, then cut it into smaller pieces before attaching it to the front of the card.
DESIGN: CANDICE CARPENTER

party 'til the cows come home

Be inspired by a whimsical chipboard shape to create an unexpected party invitation. This funny little cow takes on a party theme with the addition of a colorful party hat cut from striped patterned paper and a talk bubble for the party announcement. DESIGN: LISA STORMS

happy birthday!

Nothing says birthdays better than a gift. Disguise a plain cardstock card to create your own wrapped creation using striped and dotted patterned papers and ribbon. The front of this card is covered with one patterned paper, and a box "top" was cut from a cardstock strip and covered with a contrasting paper, then attached with adhesive foam. A ribbon wrapped from top to bottom and embellished with a gift tag completes the look. DESIGN: LISA STORMS

happy birthday!

Wishing you a purr-fect birthday!

purr-fect birthday

With a few carefully chosen embellishments, you can give your paper piecings extra spunk. Instead of simply cutting out a piece of cardstock for this cat's head, take it one step further and use adhesive strips or tape to adhere ribbon lengths to a cardstock base. Instead of cutting tiny pieces, such as parts of the face of this cat, you also can use similarly shaped embellishments like brads. The patterns are on *page 180*. DESIGN: CATHY BLACKSTONE

PAPER-PIECE WITH AN EXISTING PATTERN STEP-BY-STEP

Learn to use one of our patterns for easy paper piecing.

①　Gather your materials: pencil, pattern, cardstock, craft knife (or scissors), cutting mat, adhesive.

②　Cut out the shapes from the pattern and trace each on your desired shade of cardstock.

③　Cut out the shapes from the cardstock and assemble them on your project.

happy birthday little lady

Flowers for eyes and patterned-paper circles for spots create a fun effect on this pieced ladybug. Instead of folding, cut the card in half and sew the pieces together at one edge. Make a second row of stitches for extra durability. To finish the card, stamp a greeting on a white paper strip. DESIGN: CATHY BLACKSTONE

it's just a number

A pink branch and glittered letters give a wise owl cut from patterned paper a girlish touch. Chalking the branches, leaves, and bubble helps define the edges. To amp up the chipboard glitter letters and give it a splash of color, place cardstock in the openings of the letters.
DESIGN: CANDICE CARPENTER

you're invited

Festive yet extremely easy describes this streamer-style card. Just choose four different colored ribbons and attach one ends of each ribbon to the back side of the card front. Twist the strands over the top to the front of the card using a glue dot to secure the loops as you twist them and to attach the ends. DESIGN: LISA STORMS

you're invited

champ

This graphic birthday card is a hit for a baseball lover. Use the patterns on *page 180* to piece together a ball cap with red and navy cardstock, and add machine stitching to highlight the top layer. Or, use the patterns for the glove, kite, or ballet shoes, on *pages 180-181*, to change the theme. To make a sturdy star charm, punch and layer three cardstock stars and attach them with floss tied around the card fold. DESIGN: VALERIE SALMON

IT'S IN THE DETAILS
Add clever details to make your piecings shine.

This baseball mitt is simple to make since it consists of only two pieces. To add detail, outline the top layer with brown pen and add three types of stitches.

Tape a length of white floss to the back of the kite and attach paper bows to the string with super-tacky adhesive.

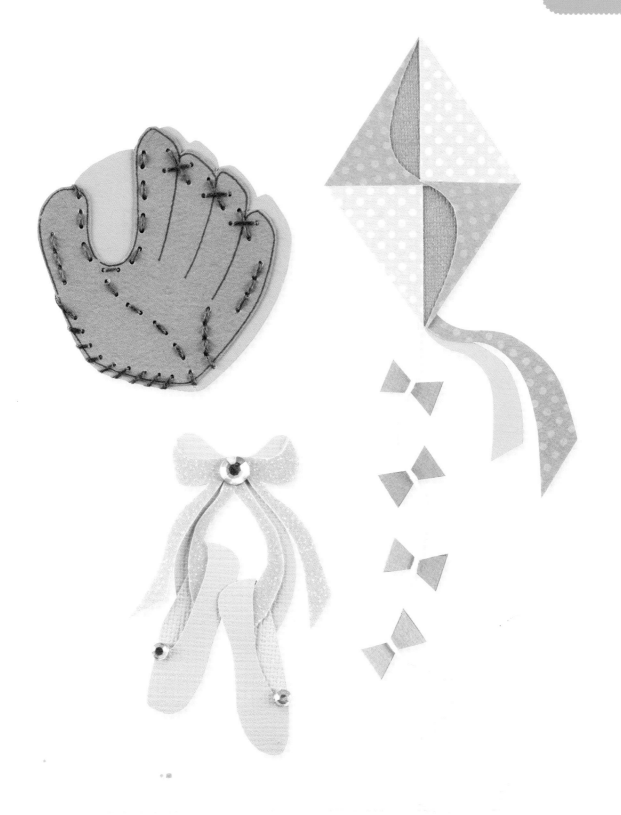

*✳ Use several tones of cardstock
to create shading.*

birthday trio

Some may call them pipe cleaners, others may describe them as chenille stems—whatever you call them, these fuzzy wired supplies can make a versatile and textural addition to your cards. To make placement easy, poke a hole in the card base for each end of the wire, then thread the pieces through and adhere or bend back the ends to the back of the card. Combine it with felt, as was done for the flowers and candle flames on the birthday cake card or bend them into shapes like on the rainbow card. DESIGNS: AMY AND ABBY LICHT

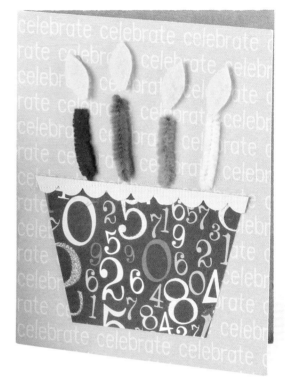

You never know when a card-giving occasion might just pop up. Be at the ready with this collection of thank-you, get-well, congratulatory, sympathy, friendship, and "just because" cards.

everyday occasions

a friend

Create a unified typographical look by combining patterned word papers with papers rubber-stamped with lettering. This friendship card uses a variety of punched and layered circles using both types. A simple alphabet stamp set can be used to spell out any word, and mixing and matching both uppercase and lowercase letters gives your card a more artistic look.
DESIGN: ROBYN WERLICH

thanks

This card is so simple to make, you'll want to make multiples to keep on hand for when the need arises. Embellish a solid cardstock rectangle with three squares punched from patterned papers and mount the whole arrangement on a vibrant colored background. Print "Thanks" in reverse onto colored cardstock, then cut out the letters using a crafts knife for a custom machine greeting. DESIGN: MEGAN BOETTCHER

celebrate

Wispy flowers give this simple card plenty of personality.
When creating your own flowers, be sure to slightly curl the
petals for added texture. Lightly sanding the edges of the
cardstock stems gives the green and orange cardstock pizzazz.
And for an unexpected touch on the inside of your card,
fold double-sided patterned paper to be the card base.

DESIGN: VICKI BOUTIN.

lots of hugs

Give a stamped card a completely different look by stamping with a medium other than ink. This abstract flower was stamped with watercolor paint, while the words were stamped with traditional stamping ink once the watercolor paint was dry. The speckled background was created by lightly tapping a brush filled with watercolor paint over the image, causing the paint to spatter.
DESIGN: JENNIFER MCGUIRE

missing you

Sometimes all you need is a little sparkle to give a card some glamour. A glittered chipboard accent frames a rub-on sentiment in the center of this narrow card. To add glitz to a plain chipboard accent, trim double-sided adhesive to fit it, adhere it to the surface, then sprinkle the tacky surface with glitter. DESIGN: ALEXIS HUNTOON

hi

Punch or cut a circle in the front of your card to let a short and sweet sentiment that's printed inside show through. Position a cute stamped image, like this owl cut from cardstock or a die cut so it peeks through the hole.

DESIGN: SHANNON TIDWELL

you're so sweet

Bypass die cuts and embellish a card front with a cutout rubber-stamped image as was done for the cherries on this card. Stamp lettering onto card strips, and dress up the design with an artificial bloom accented with a heat-embossed brad in the center. To emboss brads or other heat-resistant items, just apply ink over the surface, cover in glitter powder, and heat-set. Hold hard-to-handle items with a pair of craft tweezers.

DESIGN: ERIKIA GHUMM

smile

A large rubber stamp flower is a versatile item for creating all kinds of all-occasion cards. This particular flower was given an aged appearance with distress embossing powder—a special type of powder that has a release agent that lets you rub part of the image off after heating. Before rubbing a design, be sure to let the melted powder cool completely. To remove even more, gently scrape over the powder with a craft knife.

DESIGN: ERIKIA GHUMM

HEAT EMBOSS STEP-BY-STEP

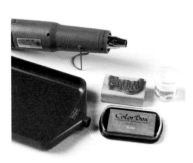

① Gather your materials: cardstock, stamp, pigment-based ink, clear embossing powder, crafts tray or scratch paper, heat tool.

② Stamp an image onto cardstock. Sprinkle embossing powder over the stamped design, and shake the excess into the crafts tray. Return the leftover powder to the container.

③ Hold the heat tool a few inches away from the cardstock and move it slowly over the stamped image to melt the embossing powder. When the powder is melted, it becomes shiny and raised.

for you

Here's a new use for a few clear buttons. Cut same-sized circles with floral motifs and position the buttons on top to make dimensional flowers. Embellish the centers with knotted ribbons, then create a bouquet on the card front by cutting stems and leaves from paper scraps from your stash. Tie the stems together with ribbon and add a mini tag for the sentiment. DESIGN: POLLY MALY

for you

hello friend

Group paper piecings together to create a three-dimensional effect on the front of a card for a special friend. Each of the elements—the bird and the cluster of branches and berries—were embossed to add subtle detail. A coordinating ribbon wrapped around the entire card front pulls it all together for a unified look. Patterns are on *page 181*. DESIGN: JENNIFER PEBBLES

you're the best

A lone white flower attached with a brad is the focus of this feel-good card. Pink trim detail outlines the flower and gives the card a pop of color, while torn paper used for the background gives it a more casual feel. Rounded edges and dotted paper contribute to a vintage vibe. DESIGN: ERICA HERNANDEZ

april showers

The pieces of this umbrella were cut from rubber-stamped paper, then centered over a pretty paper background and mounted with adhesive foam to make it pop off the page. Gems and a ribbon accent the umbrella points and handle. You can find the umbrella patterns on *page 182*. For additional designs including the butterfly, ladybug, and flower, see the patterns on *page 182*. For more information about using stamped piecings, see *below*.

DESIGN: VALERIE SALMON

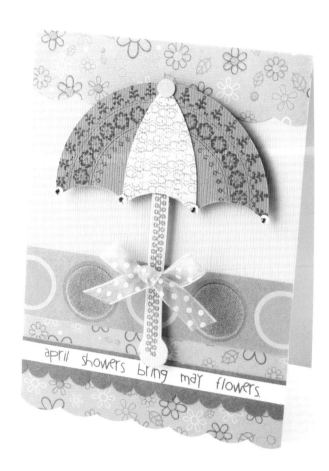

SPRUCE IT UP WITH STAMPS

Give your pieced designs subtle detail by stamping in a hue slightly darker than the paper of your piecings. Spice up your paper piecings with these stamping suggestions.

BEND THE BORDER
Acrylic border stamps allow you to move beyond the straight and narrow. Gently bend the stamps so the pattern matches the curve of your strips.

MAKE YOUR OWN
Stamp a design onto solid-color cardstock to create your own patterned paper and then cut your piecing.

FOLLOW THE LINES
Base your design on the shape of your stamps. The petals are cut out to follow the shape of the stamped design.

＊ Give your designs subtle detail
by stamping in a hue slightly darker
than the paper of your piecings.
The patterns are on *page 182*.

pretty all-purpose

Need a card for any occasion? Use up your scraps of paper and ribbon to create a simple card like this one. Adhere three strips of patterned paper to a piece of scrap paper, then trim it to size and round the four corners. Layer the rectangle under a border-punched strip of cardstock and a ribbon wrapped around the front of the card. Top it with an accent, or if you want a more personalized card, add a sentiment.

DESIGN: VALERIE SALMON

talk, rest, smile

If you find yourself with an abundance of inspirational phrase stickers, pick out a few and arrange them in a grid on the front of a card. Or use the same idea and your computer to print colored squares and words onto a piece of white cardstock. Add a dimensional sticker flower in the center to finish off the card.

DESIGN: POLLY MALY

sympathy

Express your sympathy by replacing bold patterned papers with more muted tones. Add a simple die-cut shape, like a butterfly, as an uplifting embellishment.

DESIGN: LISA STORMS

thanks a latte

Who doesn't love a cup of joe? You can re-create this steaming cup of coffee from patterned paper using the pattern on *page 183*. To make the cup stand out against the background of the card, ink the edges of the piecings before attaching them to the cardstock base. The realistic-looking stitches underneath the greeting are digital, to complement the font, but you could substitute with actual machine-stitching if you wish.

DESIGN: ERICA HERNANDEZ

woodsy mushroom

This retro-inspired mushroom motif was created using an assortment of patterned fabrics. When paired with the nature-inspired background, it creates a delightful greeting. The greeting at the bottom of the card was made with a label maker. The mushroom pattern is on *page 182*. Use our tips for backing fabric with cardstock *below*.

DESIGN: ERIKIA GHUMM

BACK YOUR FABRIC WITH CARDSTOCK STEP-BY-STEP

Backing your fabric with cardstock will make it easier to handle.

① Gather your materials: fabric, cardstock, a pen, scissors, and a sheet of adhesive paper.

② Apply the fabric to a cardstock base covered in a sheet of adhesive paper, and trace your design onto the back of the cardstock.

③ Trim your design and piece it together. The cardstock back will make it easier to adhere to your project.

you brighten my day

Experiment with color and texture by tearing brightly colored pieces of paper into heart shapes and arranging the shapes to create a flower. Stitch around the petals and use buttons for embellishments to create a unique card for someone special in your life. DESIGN: CATHY BLACKSTONE

mix-and-match thanks

Love fonts? What better way to express yourself than with a collection of your favorites to express your gratitude. Print out the expression in a multitude of colors, sizes, and fonts. You can use either photo-editing software to combine them into one page that can be printed as one piece, or print some of the sayings onto patterned papers and cut them into strips. Add mini buttons and small ribbon bows to embellish the collage.
DESIGN: HELEN NAYLOR

flowers

You might call it a split personality, but this card features two of everything. Two colors keep the look simple on two portions, while two techniques, including stamped flowers on the top and punched holes on the bottom, mix up the look. To add interest, cut out stamped images instead of stamping directly onto the card. A ribbon hides the seam between the two designs. DESIGN: MELISSA DIEKEMA

welcome home

To create a quirky housewarming card, piece a cute cottage from bold patterned paper and cardstock. A doorknob made from a brad, and a button stitched to the center of the layered felt sun lend unexpected finishing touches. Find the house pattern on *page 184*. Or substitute the deer and bird, butterfly, or owl in tree motif shown *opposite*. The patterns can be found on *pages 183 and 184*.

DESIGN: CINDY TOBEY

HOW TO PAPER-PIECE STEP-BY-STEP

① Cut out the patterns and outline each shape with a pencil. Or print the pattern on vellum, darken the lines, and trace the design onto paper using a window as a light box.

② Hand-cut the design with a craft knife over a self-healing mat. If you're not confident in your hand-cutting skills, try precision-tipped scissors for simple shapes.

③ Piece together the elements. If your piecings include tiny shapes, use adhesive that comes in pen form or adhesive dots. Embellish your finished piecing as desired.

enjoy

Before you toss any more paper scraps in the trash, pull out your punches and punch out some shapes. This assemblage of punched petals and a leaf combine to form a flower with a brad center. The lone green leaf is the perfect spot for hand writing a short greeting.

DESIGN: POLLY MALY

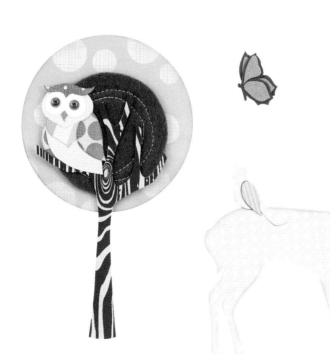

✳ Cut shapes from a variety of patterns and colors to highlight each layer.

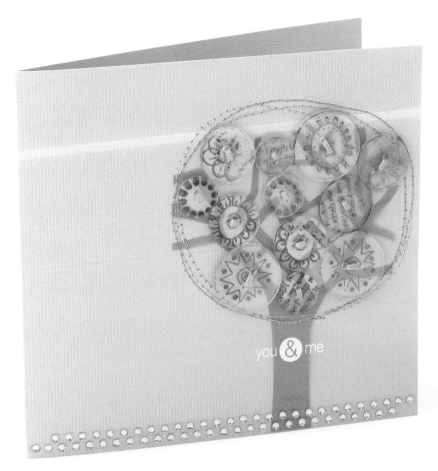

you & me

Stamping isn't just for paper anymore. Solvent inks, which are suitable for stamping onto plastic, glass, or metal, make it possible to stamp on clear buttons and create one-of-a-kind embellishments. On these examples, pretty sketch-like designs were stamped onto the buttons, then the buttons were grouped together and adhered onto a cutout tree trunk to complete the tree design.

DESIGN: TRACY KYLE

i can't say it enough

A single rubber stamp creates a big impact when repeated across strips of patterned papers. The background of this thank-you card is a great way to use up leftover strips of paper: just unify them by repeating a single, stamped message. Feature a larger stamped message on a larger piece of paper in the center, then embellish it with small buttons tied with bits of thread.

DESIGN: NIKKI KRUEGER

simple get well

Get creative with your patterned paper by transforming polka-dot paper into a bandage-themed get-well card. Trim a strip of neutral polka-dot paper, then round the corners and add a square of neutral solid paper on top for a realistic-looking bandage. Layer it over two brightly colored polka-dot papers with rounded edges, then add your sentiment with stickers on layered white cardstock and vellum circles to complete this cheerful get-well card. DESIGN: LISA STORMS

put them in stitches

Whether you prefer to stitch by hand or machine, little sewn details are a neat way to add texture to a card. DESIGNS: TRACY KYLE

1 Backdrop Buzz Create a unique background for your project by drawing the pattern first or sewing it free-form. Here, a series of straight lines stitched with variegated thread sets off the heart design. To learn how to machine-stitch, see the sidebar *opposite bottom*.

2 Fabric Fun Stitching is a no-brainer way to attach fabric to a layout. To prevent the fabric from shifting on the paper, tack it down temporarily with a small amount of adhesive.

3 Free-Form Flair Stitching by hand is easy if you lightly draw the design first and then punch small holes over the design with your sewing machine needle. The holes serve as a stitching guide.

4 Zig and Zag Attach fibers or thin ribbon with a zigzag stitch. Vary the width of the zigzag depending on the item you're stitching.

5 Forget the Thread Create a playful punched pattern by running your paper project through your sewing machine without thread. The effect is subtle but cool, and it's a super-easy technique for beginners.

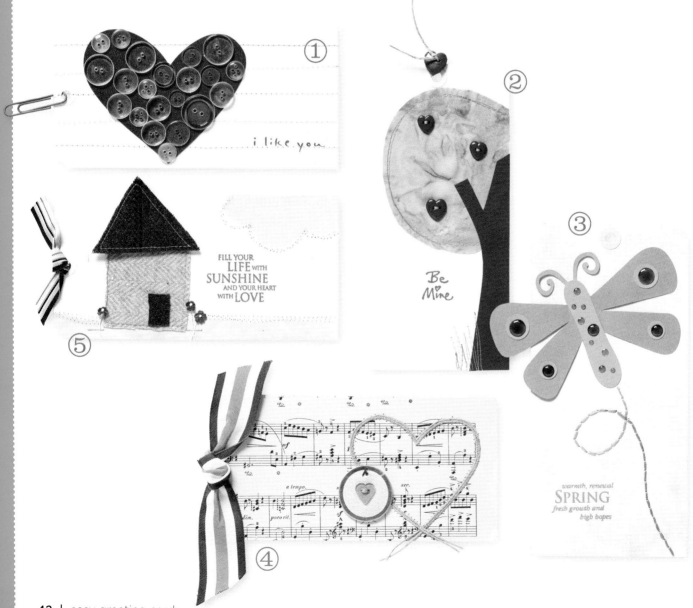

i like you

FILL YOUR LIFE WITH SUNSHINE AND YOUR HEART WITH LOVE

Be Mine

warmth, renewal
SPRING
fresh growth and
high hopes

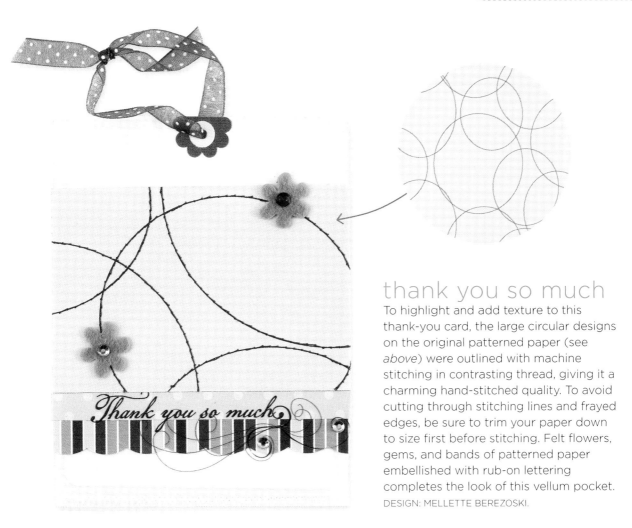

thank you so much

To highlight and add texture to this thank-you card, the large circular designs on the original patterned paper (see *above*) were outlined with machine stitching in contrasting thread, giving it a charming hand-stitched quality. To avoid cutting through stitching lines and frayed edges, be sure to trim your paper down to size first before stitching. Felt flowers, gems, and bands of patterned paper embellished with rub-on lettering completes the look of this vellum pocket.

DESIGN: MELLETTE BEREZOSKI.

MACHINE-STITCH A DESIGN STEP-BY-STEP

① Gather your materials: tag or paper, pencil, thread, machine.

② Lightly sketch your design on the cardstock.

③ Start your machine. Stitch along the pencil-drawn line. Erase the pencil marks.

grazie

The design of this thank-you card was inspired by the pattern on a leftover scrap of paper. To re-create the look, trim around circular motifs on patterned paper and mount it onto solid cardstock. For this particular card, the hand-drawn quality of the circular designs inspired the hand-doodled lines that frame the card and follow the curves of the paper cutout.

DESIGN: KATIE THORTON

thanks!

Amy made this 3-inch-square thank-you card from her stash of ribbon scraps. By keeping to a black-and-white background and white sticker letters, the hodgepodge of colorful ribbon colors work well together. The mini card is the perfect size for clipping to a gift bag, tucking into a bunch of flowers, or left as an unexpected treat on a coworker's desk.

DESIGN: AMY LICHT

you did it!

Celebrate a special accomplishment with a colorful banner made by stamping triangles and letters onto white cardstock. Cut out the pennants using decorative-edge scissors and punch two holes in each one. Assemble the banner by attaching the corners of the triangles together with brads, then add baker's twine bows to the ends. "Hang" the banner across the folded edge of your card base with glue dots. Print the rest of your greeting on an index card and punch a decorative border along one edge. DESIGN: LEAH FUNG

microbead magic

Love microbeads, but don't know how to use them? Get inspired by these ideas to add sparkle and shine to your cards and tags. DESIGNS: TRACY KYLE

1 **Shake It** Beads can be a wonderful addition to a shaker box or watch crystal. Put in plenty of colorful accents, or add just a few for a touch of color. For extra sparkle, mix in a bit of glitter with the beads. To make your own shaker box, see the sidebar *opposite bottom*.

2 **Be Edgy** Use a thin line of quick-drying liquid adhesive to accent the edge of your photos or other embellishments. For a bigger punch of color, use a thicker line of adhesive and even more beads.

3 **Bead Brads** Beads can dress up simple brads. A liquid adhesive or double-stick tape easily attaches the beads to the brad. Use the redesigned embellishment as the center of a flower, or let it shine on its own.

4 **Circular Reasoning** Cut double-stick tape into shapes or strips to adhere microbeads to homemade accents.

5 **Sticky Stuff** For a cool texture, add clear beads to a sticker using double-stick tape or clear glue. You can cover the entire surface of the sticker or use beads to highlight a specific area.

A+

Let someone know that they are the apple of your eye with this seed bead-covered apple that looks good enough to eat. The apple was first die-cut from heavyweight sheet adhesive, then covered with seed beads and embellished with a metal stem and leaf. A tiny hang tag leaves just enough room for a handwritten "A+".

DESIGN: CANDI GERSHON

MAKE A BEAD-SHAKER ACCENT STEP-BY-STEP

① Gather your materials: sticker, plastic-domed accent or watch crystal, pencil, liquid adhesive, beads.

② Trace the plastic dome on the sticker. Add liquid adhesive to the inside of the line and let it sit until it gets tacky.

③ Put the beads in the plastic dome and adhere the sticker over the top, making sure the glue lines up with the edges. Let dry.

tab talk

Index tabs are a scrapbooking supply that many cardmakers have in their stash. Find new ways to use these cool products with these inspiring card ideas. DESIGNS: CINDY TOBEY

1 Fun in the Sun Paint a collection of tabs bright yellow and arrange them in a circle with edges folded in to create a sun. Use scissors to cut into some of the tabs to vary the look.

2 Flower Power Arrange tabs with the points facing out and add a fabric strip to make a flower.

3 Sail Away Transform a single tab into the sail for a makeshift sailboat by adding zigzag stitches through the center and threading a wire through the stitches for a mast.

> ✳ Use a pencil eraser to push and pull small, hard-to-grab items into place on a card.

valentine's day

Don't forget your special Valentine this February. From romantic to kitschy, you'll find the perfect card to express your feelings for your sweetheart among this collection of easy-to-make cards.

i ♥ you

Two flower petals plucked from an artificial flower embellishment form the heart in the rub-on title of this valentine. Round the corners and ink the edges on both the base and the patterned-paper background to define the edges. Attach the remainder of the flower with a patterned paper circle for the center along with a die-cut stem to complete the card. DESIGN: LISA STORMS

hoo loves you?

Look closely at this hooty fellow and you'll realize that his eyes and beak are actually a heart. Cut this cute piecing from plaid and houndstooth patterned papers using the pattern on *page 185*, then punch circles for his eyes. Print the talk bubble using your computer, or add the lettering with rub-ons or letter stickers. DESIGN: ERIN ROE

be mine

Prove you're crazy for your valentine with a love-struck paper-pieced bird. Cathy finished the card by cutting jagged "grass" from green patterned paper and rounding the card's corners. Heart-shaped brads for the bird's eyes reinforce the valentine theme.
DESIGN: CATHY BLACKSTONE.

love

The large heart on the front of this card opens down the middle to reveal a message inside. While it looks complicated, it's easy to make using the pattern on *page 186*. Just cut and score a white cardstock base as shown on the pattern, then cover it with pretty papers. A ribbon ties the whole look (and the card) together with a bow. DESIGN: VALERIE SALMON

tweet hearts

For a round card, fold a piece of cardstock in half, then partially cut a circle using a pattern or shape cutter, making sure to leave part of the folded portion intact. Hearts cut in half with scalloped-edge scissors make great wings for bird piecings.
DESIGN: JANNA WILSON

hugs

Embrace your inner tree-hugger with a valentine using large punched circles for a treetop and cork paper for a tactile tree trunk. Add dimension to the treetop with brads, and don't forget your heart-felt greeting on the trunk. The pattern is on *page 184.* DESIGN: TRACY KYLE

feb 14

Craft a lyrical card for a music lover using patterned paper inspired by vintage sheet music. To tone down the contrast of the pattern, try brushing a thin coat of white paint over the paper. Be sure to let the paint dry before randomly arranging patterned paper hearts and a rubber-stamped date on top. Finish the card edge with a line of machine stitching at the fold. DESIGN: CATHY BLACKSTONE

love always

Stitching is a budget-friendly accent when you're making valentine cards in bulk. For this card, a large heart was sketched in the center of the pink paper, then the outline was machine-stitched several times. A hand-cut, patterned-paper heart is featured inside the large stitched heart.

DESIGN: JENNIFER PERKS

LINE UP A PATTERN USING ACETATE STEP-BY-STEP

When you want to use a certain portion of your paper, use acetate to help you line up a pattern.

① Gather your materials: paper, acetate, scissors, a permanent marker, and a pencil.

② Lay the acetate over your pattern and trace the shape. Then trim around the outline.

③ Position your acetate shape over the portion of the patterned paper you want to use. Trace the design, cut it out, and erase any remaining pencil marks.

lollipop valentine

A greeting has never tasted as sweet as this lollipop-turned-valentine. To make one, layer a punched circle over a scalloped circle with adhesive foam. Attach the circles to the front of a plastic-wrapped lollipop, add another scalloped circle to the back, and embellish. Use an adhesive dot to secure the ribbon leaves. DESIGN: LISA STORMS

Put lollipop cards on display by drilling holes in a wooden block and adding fringed cardstock to mimic grass.

I pick you Valentine!

be mine

will you?

be mine . . . will you?

Cut way-cool swirls from patterned paper for a graphic touch for this valentine. Use a circle cutter to measure the rings or trace the shapes from household items such as cups and bowls. Punctuate the center of the rings with a small circle embellished with a rub-on saying, then add the second part of your greeting with another rub-on in the lower right corner of the card.

DESIGN: ERIN ROE

bee mine

Vellum wings add a realistic touch to this paper-pieced bumblebee. Add small lengths of wire for the antennae and secure tiny paper hearts to the ends. To create the bee's flight path, lightly pencil a curved line, then pierce holes along the guide and stitch them with black embroidery floss. DESIGN: JENNIFER PERKS

MAKE IT WORK

Give your paper piecings working parts with these techniques. Patterns are on *page 184*.

To make the bumblee bobble on the card, fold a strip of cardstock accordion-style and adhere one end to the card and the other end to the back of the piecing.

For the cupcake above, print a secret message on a small strip of cardstock, then top it with a glittered heart. To hide the message, cut a small slit in the cupcake's frosting and insert the cardstock strip.

whale you be mine?

Take a tongue-in-cheek approach to your valentine card crafting by letting a sticker be the inspiration for your greeting. A whale sticker mounted on cardstock and positioned behind cardstock trimmed with a wave border punch is the perfect scenario for posing the question "Whale you be mine?" The dozen punched hearts forming the whale's spout reinforces the love theme. DESIGN: LISA STORMS

love

Express your love this Valentine's Day with a collection of hearts punched from scraps of patterned paper and arranged on cardstock. When it comes to arranging, don't let the card edge stop you, simply trim the hearts flush with the card edges. Complete the card with an eye-catching sentiment like the "Love" die-cut from cardstock and secured using adhesive foam. DESIGN: TRACY KYLE

be mine

Return to your younger years by borrowing an elementary school technique to make this folded-heart card. Start by folding patterned-paper rectangles in half and cutting out simple symmetrical hearts, then cutting out the centers to make nesting heart outlines. Attach the hearts to the card base by machine-stitching along the hearts' folds, giving the greeting three-dimensional flair. DESIGN: JENNIFER PERKS

i ♥ you

Metal-rim tags are a unique way to frame words for this banner-style card. Use your computer to print your message onto pink paper, then use a circle punch to cut out the words. String the tags with baker's twine by threading the twine through heart buttons, then adhering the buttons to the top of each tag. DESIGN: VALERIE SALMON

XOXO

A simple heart die cut backed with patterned paper and framed with a scalloped-edged circle makes a striking focal point on this otherwise neutral card. Stamps make quick work of the script and greeting, while a wide ribbon dresses it up.

DESIGN: KELLY RASMUSSEN

candy bar tags

Manila hang tags from the office supply store make excellent gift tags. These tags were stamped with Valentine messages, flourishes, romantic script lettering, and even dimensional ribbon flowers for a sophisticated embellishment that's the perfect size for attaching to a purchased candy bar. DESIGNS: SANDE KRIEGER

love you

A combination of gray and cream paper layers makes a striking backdrop to a simple ticket and die-cut accent. Neutral stitching around the edges of each of the paper layers subtly frames each piece while also serving as a means of attachment. To avoid stitching through thick layers of papers, stitch each piece to the layer underneath it in pairs. Then glue the stitched pairs together to create the layered look.

DESIGN: CATHY BLACKSTONE

you're hot

With its cheeky greeting, this red-hot card would boost anyone's ego. To create the pouch, layer a square of recycled plastic on top of lined notepaper and machine-stitch a square around the edges, leaving a small opening for the candies. Place a few Red Hots through the opening, then close it up by stitching back and forth.

DESIGN: CATHY BLACKSTONE

we're a great pear

Create a pun with your title and design for a valentine with a sense of humor. Use the pear patterns on *page 185* to cut patterned paper for the fruit, then use a hand punch to create heart-shaped seeds and mount them with adhesive foam. Add a cardstock stem and a rub-on title to complete the card. DESIGN: LISA STORMS

i'll love you forever

If romantic and old-fashioned define your valentine card tastes, you'll love this vintage-inspired card. A distressed patterned paper and decorative-edged journaling card look weathered yet sophisticated as the background for pretty felt flowers. A twine-tied sentiment reinforces the down-home feel, and small gems add a touch of sparkle.

DESIGN: RHONDA BONIFAY

I'll love you
forever

property of:

Hearts don't have to be pretty and full of flourishes. This heart is crafted using two overlapping tags to make an edgy shape. You can make your own tags by using your photo-editing software to print two red rectangles with white messages, trimming off two corners, and punching a hole at the top of each one. Define the tag edges with ink and add hole reinforcement stickers and twine to each hole before attaching the tags to a card base.
DESIGN: ERIN ROE

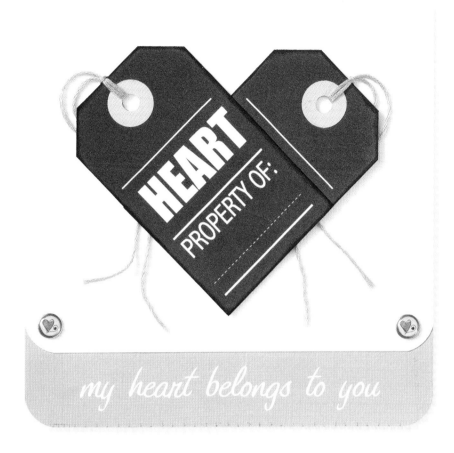

my heart belongs to you

i ♥ you

Repurpose plastic packaging on a cute-as-can-be shaker card with a hidden message. Start by printing the greeting, then layer a heart frame cut from foam over it. Pour sequins in the middle of the foam heart, glue plastic over the foam, and top it with a heart frame. For step-by-step instructions on making a shaker box, see *page 47*. DESIGN: JENNIFER PERKS

you're sweet

Since life is like a box of chocolates, why not make a few sweet pieces from paper for your valentine? Use the patterns on *page 185* to make these frilly confections, and use a crimper to add a realistic touch to the scallop-edged wrappers for each chocolate. Add tiny rhinestones, mini brads, and small paper strips to embellish the tops of each treat. Use the patterns on *page 185* to make a heart-shaped candy box, envelope, and square chocolate, too.

DESIGN: VALERIE SALMON

wood you be mine?

To create the texture on the base of this clever card, a wood-grain pattern was embossed onto brown cardstock using a texture plate, then the raised areas were inked to help the texture stand out. A bird die cut, piece of patterned paper, and letter stickers simply embellish the greeting. If you look closely, you might notice that the question mark is actually a "P" sticker with a piece snipped from it.

DESIGN: LISA STORMS

candy bar robot

Turn a mini candy bar into a robot by wrapping it in patterned paper and adding a head, arms, and legs. Give each robot its own personality and style by playing around with different buttons, punches, and papers. DESIGN: LISA STORMS

tiny cards

Create a set of 2×2-inch cards and envelopes for all the valentines on your list. Arm yourself with a hand-held heart punch and a few rubber stamps and you'll have enough for everyone on your list in no time. DESIGNS: ROBYN WERLICH

spring holidays

Spring ushers in flowers, green grass, and balmy days, but also some of our favorite holidays. Remember someone special with a spring-time greeting to wish them a happy Easter, Mother's Day, or Father's Day.

bunny

Paper-piece this hoppy bunny using the pattern on *page 187*.
For a tactile touch and fuzzy appearance, apply white flock to
his cheeks, tummy, and tail pieces before assembling the pieces.
Attach egg-shaped brads to a thin cardstock strip strung to his
hands, or fold the bunny's arms in for a hug-ready pose.

DESIGN: JENNIFER PERKS

happy easter

Welcome Easter with a bloom created by layering scallop-edged circles punched from pink and orange cardstock scraps. On top, a white punched circle is embellished with a dark pink flower that was created using a flocking kit, producing a design with a fuzzy feel. The stem is a portion of a wavy border sticker and the greeting is stamped and glittered.

DESIGN: MICHELLE RUBIN

easter blessings

A large title spelled out with green acrylic letters fills an 8×3½-inch card nicely. Before you toss your pretty pastel scraps, cut them into narrow strips to make a simple but colorful border. Apply a rub-on greeting to white cardstock and layer it over the large letters with adhesive foam to make it stand out against the background. DESIGN: MELISSA INMAN

birds

Frills and lace needn't be reserved just for your Easter best. Apply a fancy laser-cut paper to a butter yellow cardstock background to make the background for this Easter card. Two bird images stamped onto white cardstock and colored with watercolor pencils are then matted and mounted in the center of the card.

DESIGN: MICHELLE RUBIN

USE WATERCOLOR PENCILS STEP-BY-STEP

Blend watercolor pencils for a hand-painted effect.

①Gather your materials: watercolor pencils, paintbrush, and accent you want to color.

②Color in parts of your image—a little color goes a long way.

③Run a wet paintbrush over the pencil lines, and brush the color into the empty areas. Use two colors for a stronger blended effect.

egg-specially for you

For a super-simple Easter card, frame a die cut with a clear acrylic frame. To make the pairing more interesting, place the frame a bit off-kilter. Layer the title treatment for a more pleasing arrangement. To compensate for the overlap with the thick frame, prop up the other side of the title treatment with adhesive foam.

DESIGN: MELISSA INMAN

happy easter

This small card was easily created using a plain chipboard shape and covering it with a striking patterned paper. When covering complicated chipboard shapes, use spray adhesive to attach the paper to the chipboard (don't worry about the shape of the paper yet). Then use a crafts knife to trim the excess paper around the outer edges and inside any openings within the shape. Before adhering the shape to the card, attach a small tag with an Easter greeting written on it to the shape using a small length of ribbon.

DESIGN: MELISSA INMAN

easter wishes

Six squares and a rectangular title make up the simple grid design of this Easter card. Of the six squares, three are Easter-themed square stickers mounted on paper and three are punched patterned-paper squares. Together, they are all arranged in an alternating pattern. The stickers are slightly elevated using adhesive foam.
DESIGN: MELISSA INMAN

hippity hoppity

This large Easter-themed sticker could have stood alone on this card, but it would have seemed pretty plain. Leftover patterned-paper scraps trimmed into uneven strips and adhered to the card front creates a vertically striped background for the sticker instead.
DESIGN: MELISSA INMAN

there's nobunny quite like you

Diagonally striped paper gives this simple Easter card an extra burst of springtime energy. The front flap is punched with a circle to create an opening for a bunny accent to peek through from the inside of the card. To complete the look, top the card with a green brad and an adorable printed sentiment, "There's nobunny quite like you." DESIGN: MELISSA INMAN

hoppy easter

Shake up your card making by modifying the shape of your cards. Instead of the usual rectangle shape, this square card frames a large, round bunny sticker nicely. To make the sticker stand out against the background, mount it onto a coordinating colored circle. Print the title onto white cardstock, but print the "o" in "hoppy" green to show off the spelling change, and attach it with colored brads. DESIGN: MELISSA INMAN

you are the greatest

The only paper you'll need for this Mother's Day card is the cardstock to create the folded base. Buttons both attach and embellish the grouping of artificial flowers to the card front, and hand-stitched stems extend out from underneath the blooms. Twill ribbon gives the illusion that the bouquet is tied together.

DESIGN: CANDI GERSHON

mother

Punched shapes, scalloped edges, and a ribbon detail give this Mother's Day card a playful personality. To give the card a bit of dimension, try elevating elements or bending pieces, such as the wings on the butterfly shown here, and adding gems to the design, as was done for the butterfly body and with the letter sticker greeting.

DESIGN: VALERIE SALMON

we ♥ you mom

For a streamlined design, use your computer to create a collage-like card. Digital papers from a kit were used to create this heartfelt card and were combined with playful embellishments, such as the flower that fills the center of the "o" in "mom."

DESIGN: KIM CROTHERS

happy mother's day

Think outside of the sewing box when it comes to creating clever, handmade cards. The birds on this Mother's Day card have button bodies embellished with googly eyes, patterned paper, feathers, and stamped curlicues. Sequins around a chipboard branch create shiny leaves, and a stapled greeting covers up a stamping mistake.

DESIGN: CATHY BLACKSTONE

BACK CLEAR BUTTONS WITH PAPER STEP-BY-STEP

Turn clear buttons into coordinating accents.

① Gather your materials: clear buttons, patterned paper, clear-drying adhesive, craft knife, foam brush.

② Apply a small amount of adhesive to the back of the button. Lay the button on top of the patterned paper and press it down firmly to eliminate any trapped air bubbles.

③ When the adhesive is dry, carefully trim the excess paper away from the button with a craft knife.

you are the best

A cool color scheme and a textural backdrop provides the basis for this nature-inspired Mother's Day card. The dotted background paper for the top portion of the card is embossed. A menagerie of chipboard accents, including an owl, flowers, and leaves complete this outdoor-loving greeting. DESIGN: LESLIE LIGHTFOOT

happy mother's day

A pretty handmade medallion makes a striking statement on this card and looks as pretty as a purchased embellishment. To make your own, print the sentiment on patterned paper, punch it into a circle, and layer it over two scalloped circles. To add a little shimmer, cover the largest scalloped circle with glitter before layering the other pieces on top. Attach the entire piece with adhesive foam to elevate it on the patterned paper background. DESIGN: LEAH FUNG

✱ Make paper-pieced jewelry more durable by constructing it out of heavyweight cardstock.

happy mother's day

Add a removable element to a Mother's Day card that doubles as a gift. The three-dimensional flower on the front of this simple card is actually pinned to the card, making it a removable piece of jewelry. The pattern for the flower is on *page 187*. Make the flower extra-durable by constructing it out of heavyweight cardstock.

DESIGN: ERIN ROE

happy mother's day mi mi

What could be more appropriate for Mom than colorful flowers on her Mother's Day card? Each of these flowers were punched from scraps, and their edges were distressed by a gentle rubbing with sandpaper. The flowers were arranged in two vertical rows, with a computer-printed sentiment added into one of the spaces. Rather than struggling to stitch the buttons through the thick layers of the card, use adhesive dots to secure the buttons (which were threaded with wire) to the card instead.
DESIGN: ERIN CLARKSON

happy mother's day

A diminuitive size, subdued colors, and patterned papers make this a fun-loving card for any mother. The chipboard frame resembles a postage stamp, making it a great backdrop for creating your own collage for expressing your love and appreciation.
DESIGN: ERIN CLARKSON

thank you mom

Die-cut paper is an easy way to instantly accessorize a card. For this card, a die-cut sheet was trimmed to fit the top of the card base, using the curved edge as part of the design. A metal bookplate frames the greeting, adding dimension and vibrant color, while stickers and brads accent the die-cut pattern.

DESIGN: ERICA HERNANDEZ

thank you mom

grandma

A scalloped edge adds interest to the first flap of this Mother's Day card's tri-fold design. Start with a wide rectangular piece of cardstock for the card base, then fold it into thirds. Trim the left flap with decorative-edge scissors, then add patterned paper, embellishments, and a printed greeting for a fresh look.

DESIGN: MELLETTE BEREZOSKI

Grandma
[PERFECT JUST THE WAY YOU ARE]

mom

Add pizzazz to your Mother's Day card this year with a variety of textural embellishments. Chipboard accents, felt flowers, and sparkly gems make this one a keeper.

DESIGN: VALERIE SALMON

FAKE A PUNCH STEP-BY-STEP

Use a punch to cut a shape from unpunchable fabric or felt.

① Punch a simple shape from sturdy cardstock.

② Trace the shape onto felt (or chipboard, foam, etc.) with a marker.

③ Hand-cut the shape from the material.

thanks, dad

An embellished tie is the focal point of this Father's Day card. To give the cardstock tie a patterned look, stamp stars onto small cardstock scraps and place brads through the centers. Cut out the stars and adhere them to the tie.

DESIGN: VICKI BOUTIN

happy father's day

The patterned-paper grid on this Father's Day card gives it a clean-cut yet masculine feel. Handyman icons (cut from patterned paper), stickers, and chalk are the basis for this perfect card for the do-it-yourself man in your life. DESIGN: JAMI BLACKHAM

well-dressed

A pieced shirt, tie, and suit jacket placed on a computer-printed background expresses a child's sentiment to a father on this card. Print part of the background greeting in a color to match the color of the tie. DESIGN: CHRISTINA COLE

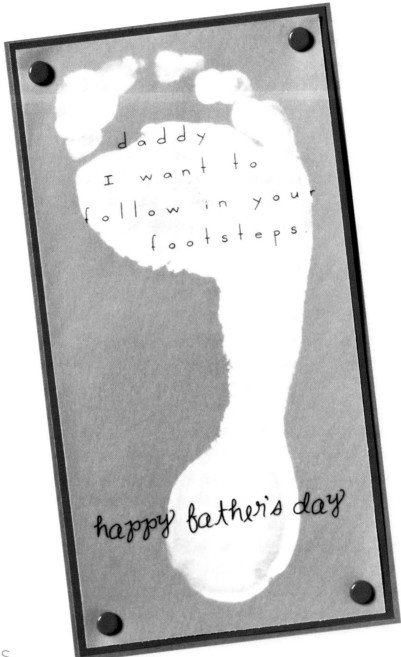

daddy
I want to
follow in your
footsteps.

happy father's day

baby's footprint

A stamp of Baby's footprint will send a message straight to Dad's heart. White paint printed the footprint onto dark blue cardstock, which was then mounted on light blue. A heartfelt message was printed on vellum, and all three layers were secured with brads. DESIGN: KATHLEEN PANEITZ AND POLLY MALY

graduations

Celebrate years of hard work and dedication with a graduation card fit for the favorite teen in your life. From open house invites, congratulatory cards, and gift-card holders, you'll find just the right one to fit your student's personality.

grad

Graduation cards don't have to be all about caps, gowns, and diplomas. Whimsical punched butterflies flutter among the word "grad" for a more seasonal look on this graduation card. To add interest to the word, large letters die-cut from graduation-themed patterned paper are positioned so that one letter is shifted above the others. The butterfly wings are bent slightly up to give them a dimensional look, and gems highlight the wings. DESIGN: LISA STORMS

it's time to . . . celebrate

Avoid the extra pressure of handcrafted invitations and design an easy-to-print digital variety. If you're mailing the cards, it's always a good idea to verify standard postal sizes to ensure a smooth printing and mailing process. Or, avoid postage altogether and e-mail the invites to everyone on your list. DESIGN: SANDE KRIEGER

please join us

Combine a classic invitation design with pops of vibrant color for a teen-worthy result. For a feminine touch, add an elegant ribbon and gems. When adding ribbon to a single piece of cardstock on a layered design, cut a slit on each side of the cardstock and pull the ribbon ends through, reducing lumps while securing the pieces. DESIGN: MELANIE LOUETTE

follow your dreams...

Recent graduates always appreciate gift cards, so why not personalize one with a handcrafted card holder with style? This greeting houses a removable gift-card holder complete with pockets for cards (or memorabilia and photos once the gift cards have been used). For extra durability, construct this gift with cardstock and heavyweight patterned paper.

DESIGN: SHERI REGULY

Open the card to reveal the gift.

Create a box fold at the top edge of the card to leave room for the trifold gift-card holder.

Include a tri-fold gift-card holder.

* Tie a string through two eyelets to secure the gift-card holder to the card base.

MAKE A GIFT-CARD HOLDER STEP-BY-STEP

① Gather your materials: cardstock, patterned paper, adhesive, eyelets, and string.

② Fold a 9×4-inch piece of cardstock in thirds.

③ Adhere a 3×2½-inch piece of patterned paper to all but one panel, applying adhesive on just three sides to create a pocket. Add a strip of scalloped cardstock to the top of each pocket.

④ Embellish the pockets and front panel as desired, then add gift cards, photos, or a message to the grad.

⑤ Set two eyelets about 3¼ inches apart on the inside of the graduation card. Run the string through the eyelets and tie it in a bow, then tuck the gift-card holder under the string.

fold		fold	
	3×2½"	3×2½"	

conGRADs

Owl-patterned paper inspired both a border and the central embellishment on this graduation card. Placed on top of a notebook-paper background, a singled-out bird is highlighted by a punched circle and a graduation cap sticker. Two letter sticker styles combine to form the word "conGRADs"—with one style used to spell out the secondary word all in caps. DESIGN: LISA STORMS

reach for the stars

Notebook-patterned paper may recall note taking in class, but it also provides a subtle background to the layered stars on the front of this card. The stars are punched in a variety of sizes from an assortment of leftover papers, then layered with adhesive foam and placed in a pleasing arrangement on the front of the card. DESIGN: LISA STORMS

congratulations

This oblong, folded card is designed to mimic a rolled-up diploma. The extra-wide design is finished with a small sticker title and embellishment in the corner, then tied up with a bold ribbon. When designing an oversize card, consider your mailing options. This card was designed so that it would fit into a standard business-size envelope. DESIGN: LISA STORMS

so proud

Use a collage of stickers as a focal point with cap and gown stickers. The blue stickers pop off the orange patterned paper background and a blue decorative-edge border is secured with orange brads to continue the color scheme. DESIGN: VICKI BOUTIN

you rock...thanks!

Make good manners cool by crafting a set of spunky thank-you cards for your grad to send. The front of this card is easy to create in multiples by using a die-cutting tool to cut the star and the words. These cards also make a great gift for grads, or you can modify the greeting to make cards for grads to keep in touch with friends and family. DESIGN: MARY MACASKILL

congratulations

Celebrate your favorite grad's wise ways with this quick stamped card. The owl is stamped, then cut out and backed with a darker patterned paper to make it stand out. A pieced cardstock cap placed on top of the owl's head defines the graduation theme. Polka dots and a congratulatory sentiment at the bottom of the card are also stamped.

DESIGN: VICKI BOUTIN

hitch your wagon to a star

Use an inspirational quote as a theme for a congratulatory card for a recent graduate. Print your chosen quote onto white cardstock, trim it into a strip, then snip each word apart and attach each one separately to the card. To acknowledge the source of the quote without tarnishing the design, give credit on the back of the card.

DESIGN: JENNIFER PERKS

wooo whooo!

Simple oval and circle shapes are assembled and layered to create this cute owl paper piecing. Talk bubbles add to the playfulness of the design. For extra detail, add hand-drawn lines on the tree branch. DESIGN: JENNIFER PERKS

hooray!

Layers of patterned paper make this graduation card ribbon worthy. A stamped circle and ribbon strips add unexpected detail to the quick-and-easy design. To avoid an overwhelming design, a concise color scheme of blue, yellow, and green gives it a playful but unified look.
DESIGN: VICKI BOUTIN

PLEASE JOIN US

JHA

please join us as we
celebrate the graduation of
[...] ALLEN HERNANDEZ
from grand blanc high school
saturday, june 26, 2010
at 3 PM

please join us

Simple printed text and an easy-to-assemble paper piecing make this invitation a cinch to produce en masse. The pattern is on *page 183*. Incorporate the grad's school colors by matching text colors, cardstock, and a pieced accent. Add more personalization with a monogram. Traditional monogram format includes the last initial in larger type between the first and middle initial. DESIGN: ERICA HERNANDEZ

Ted is a graduate!
Join us for his graduation party

May 30, 2008
5:30 p.m.
at our home

Please bring a 4x6" photo
of you and the new grad
for his scrapbook.

ted is a graduate!

When it comes to making multiple invites, keeping it simple is the name of the game. For this invitation, a small piece of ribbon and a tag printed with the school symbol embellish the seam between a favorite photo and printed text. A double mat adds interest while keeping the workload light and the expenses low. DESIGN: JEN LESSINGER

Ted will head off to the
University of Kentucky
Aug. 22.

Send cookies:
**Memorial Hall
Room 1437B
Lexington, KY
30582**

See if he's going to
class:
555-555-5555

Forward fun e-mail:
teddd###@1.edu

Keep up with him or
MySpace:
myspace/tedba

And be sure to po
him on Faceboo

KEEP
IN touch

DESIGN: MOO.COM

* Let guests know how they can stay in touch with the graduate by giving out mini calling cards as party favors. Use a photo, your own digital design, or an online design to make your cards. Include the graduate's new address, blog, e-mail address, and maybe even mention of the grad's favorite cookies (hint, hint).

Whether you're congratulating newlyweds, a couple on their anniversary, or are looking for stationery for your own wedding, this collection of cards and invitations is brimming with elegance and sophistication.

weddings

so happy for you

A beautiful stamped flower accented with embossing powder and small gems makes a pretty backdrop for a die-cut monogram on this congratulatory card. The card front is divided into two halves, with the stamped flower on one side and printed vellum on the other. Machine-stitched edges add textural interest to the design. DESIGN: ROBYN WERLICH

b&c

Celebrate the union of two people by highlighting their initials on a metal-rimmed tag. The tag is stamped with a wedding cake motif, and letter stickers on either side of the cake feature each person's first initial. Wedding-themed ribbon is threaded through the tag and secured on the backside of the card front.

DESIGN: CATHY BLACKSTONE

kate & kevin

Save time creating an elegant background for an invitation by choosing embossed cardstock. This simple design features a rounded tab printed with the couple's names and wedding date. A ribbon wrapped around the card brings a splash of color to the design.

DESIGN: TRACY KYLE

Kate & Kevin
August 20, 2011

congratulations on saying

i do

Use chipboard letters in subdued colors to spell out a wedding sentiment. A pink chipboard heart between the words reinforces the romantic theme. A scalloped border along the bottom card edge makes a pretty finishing touch. For instructions on glittering your own chipboard letters, see *below*. DESIGN: ERIN CLARKSON

COVER CHIPBOARD WITH GLITTER STEP-BY-STEP
Enhance a chipboard die cut with sparkles.

① Gather your materials: painted chipboard, foam brush, glitter, wet glue, dimensional adhesive.

② Brush glue onto the chipboard. Sprinkle dry glitter over the chipboard and shake off the excess.

③ Cover the glitter with dimensional adhesive.

true

Love decorative edges? Put your passion into motion making this wedding card brimming with interesting edges. An elongated patterned-paper rectangle trimmed with scallops and other fancy edges fills the center of the card front. A sticker-embellished cardstock oval sentiment is also accented with a scalloped oval and chipboard hearts.
DESIGN: JANNA WILSON

happily ever after

Color empty spaces of a digital element using a colored pencil to create an image that pops. This flower was printed onto kraft cardstock, the blooms were filled in with white pencil, then the colored areas were covered with a glitter pen to lend a bit of sparkle. Tiny self-adhesive white gems were added for the flower centers. DESIGN: LUCY ABRAMS

we're tying the knot

Tie simple double knots randomly onto string to add texture and put a clever spin on a wedding announcement. Keep strings in place by hooking them onto a punched scalloped border at the top and bottom of a piece of cardstock. Put the wedding details on the inside of the card to keep the front simple and uncluttered.

DESIGN: LISA STORMS

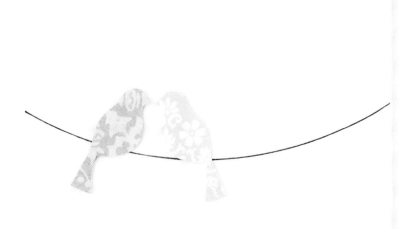

Lauren Allen

lovebirds
Perch two die-cut lovebirds on a hand-drawn telephone wire for a simple yet elegant wedding invitation. Choose coordinating tone-on-tone patterned papers in contrasting colors for each bird, and finish the card with the couple's names printed in a simple script font and a strip cut from a page of a salvaged book. DESIGN: LISA STORMS

save the date
Stamp a graphic "Save the Date" and tie in your wedding hues by coloring the design with blendable markers. A torn edge at the bottom of the stamped paper adds interest, and a matching colored ribbon below the stamped graphic holds the color scheme together. DESIGN: TRACY KYLE

USING THE LETTERPRESS STEP-BY-STEP

① Gather your materials: desktop letterpress machine with accessories (the machine featured is the Epic Six die-cutting tool), ink, brayer and plate designs, adhesive sheets, paper.

② Choose the printing plate. Remove one side of the adhesive sheet liner and place the plate on the adhesive. Trim excess adhesive.

③ Remove the liner from the back of the plate and position the plate on the clear lid of the letterpress, using the grid as a guide if needed.

congratulations

The letterpress technique prints designs and words by actually pressing the elements onto cardstock. The result is a beautiful textural effect that begs to be touched. Thanks to desktop letterpress equipment, you can create your own letterpress designs, such as these congratulations cards. Print them in batches and keep them on hand for whenever the need arises. See the instructions *below* for more information on creating your own letterpress designs.

④ Position the paper on the grid, using the plate for reference.

⑤ Once you've decided where the paper should be, stick placement guides next to the paper so you can easily place paper in the same location for multiple printings.

⑥ Apply a small amount of ink to the ink base. Remember that a little bit of ink goes a long way.

⑦ Roll the brayer over the ink until the brayer is evenly covered.

⑧ Roll ink over the plate, being careful to apply it evenly.

⑨ Close the plate lid, then roll the letterpress through the die-cutting tool.

husband and wife

You don't have to spend your time hand-cutting a lacy design when laser-cut paper makes it so easy to create a beautifully detailed card. The laser-cut floral paper on the front of this card is accented with a glittered border and a silk flower with a pearl center. DESIGN: VALERIE SALMON

love, honor, cherish

This design works well for invites or congratulatory cards. Make multiples easily by creating a circle of text in word processing software and printing several on a sheet. Flip a circle punch upside down to center the text perfectly before punching out the accent.
DESIGN: VALERIE SALMON

congrats on tying the knot

This wedding card has an air of whimsy in its design. Playing off the words "congrats on tying the knot," string wraps around the edges of scallop-edge patterned paper and is, in fact, tied in a knot. The sentiment is printed and trimmed into strips and finished off with a tiny pink heart. DESIGN: LISA STORMS

stationery set

You could pay a small fortune for custom-made letterpress wedding stationery, or you could make a small investment in desktop equipment and make your own. This collection of save the date, invitation and RSVP, thank-you, and place cards features vellum overlays and contrasting stitched details, which hold the layers together.

DESIGN: ERICA HERNANDEZ

Save the Date
john and sarah
saturday, august 28, 2010
five o'clock pm

RSVP

m _____
_____ will attend

Love

please join us
as we celebrate the marriage of

john william
and
sarah elizabeth

saturday, august 28, 2010
five o'clock pm

st mary's church

тнank you

mr & mrs
samuel jackson

NO.12

it's your happily ever after

A big, soft bow punctuates the center of this sophisticated gatefold design. The card base itself is cut from embossed paper for a subtle textural background, and is accented by a large-scale patterned paper band that slides over the base to hold it closed. The printed greeting is secured below the ribbon using pearl brads. DESIGN: JANNA WILSON

mr. & mrs.

This lighthearted wedding card is constructed from supplies that you might not immediately think of when it comes to your card making: foam stamps, acrylic paint, and glaze. Pen outlines highlight the painted letters, and a silver glaze brushed over the entire design adds interest. DESIGN: CATHY BLACKSTONE

wedding

For a more vintage-inspired look, choose a dried-flower sticker as the primary accent for a wedding card. Attach the flower sticker onto a layered cardstock rectangle printed with a wedding-themed definition, and add machine-stitched detail. Mount the rectangle onto a raw-edge silk ribbon and tie it around a cardstock base. DESIGN: ALISON BEACHEM

eternity

An elegant bridal sticker and a script-style rub-on makes it easy to create a stunning wedding card. This card includes a wide satin ribbon wrapped around the folded card and threaded underneath the matted stickers, which serves as a pretty closure when tied into a bow. DESIGN: ALISON BEACHEM

to have and to hold

Incorporate something old into a wedding card by repurposing a page from a vintage book. Use the piece as patterned paper to back a decorative block housing your sentiment and a coordinating fabric flower. Cut the leaf from contrasting patterned paper and add a printed sentiment and punched heart to complete the design.

DESIGN: LISA STORMS

celebrate

Elegant embossed paper is a natural for a wedding card. Forming the card base, the embossed paper is embellished with a band of patterned paper and a sheer ribbon. A glittery flower accented with a pearl brad center and a sticker sentiment complete the look. DESIGN: VALERIE SALMON

true love

Lace-patterned paper lends itself perfectly to the design of a wedding card. Put it to work by layering it over white cardstock for a beautiful embossed look. This quick, simple effect provides a big impact with very little effort. Add a greeting with a sticker or die-cut label. DESIGN: LISA STORMS

l-o-v-e

This tone-on-tone card is a vision in pastel blue and is an elegant way to congratulate newlyweds. The two-tone cardstock has sanded edges, and the sentiment is spelled out with metal mailbox letters. A painted metal heart charm is secured to coordinating ribbon with a small safety pin.
DESIGN: ERIN CLARKSON

best wishes

Even small embellishments can shine on a card front when dressed up properly. Use leftover patterned paper strips to boost a die-cut bouquet's presence by overlapping them into a frame. Add pen details to the strips for extra definition, and add a sticker embellishment for the greeting. DESIGN: NIKKI KRUEGER

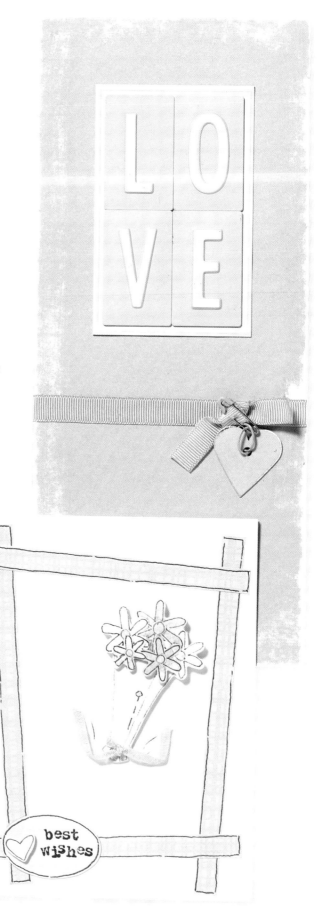

happily ever after

This pretty card mixes both soft and hard accents in a simple yet elegant design. The bottom cardstock layer has two horizontal slits cut in the top half of the piece, where a fabric paper rectangle slides through for a woven effect. Stitching around the fabric paper frames the design, and white ribbon threaded through a silver buckle is finished with a white handwritten tag. Silver brads secure a trio of tissue-paper flowers along the side of the card. DESIGN: NICHOL MAGOUIRK

silver wedding anniversary

Two die-cut love birds convey an anniversary message for the front of this pocket-style anniversary invitation. Inside the pocket is a computer-printed tag topped with a ribbon pull. Ribbon also dresses up the edge of the pocket, while subtle shading along the bird, pocket, and tag edges gives everything dimension.

DESIGN: LUCY ABRAMS

help us celebrate

Celebrate a special anniversary with a stunning card featuring a pretty field of flowers. A reverse-image stamp was used to create the image, then heat-embossing and blended distress inks give it a two-tone look. A ribbon and twine band topped with matching buttons complements the design.

DESIGN: TRACY KYLE

Help us Celebrate 30 years!

babies

A new little bundle of joy is always cause for celebration! Send your wishes of love and happiness with these cards for births and adoptions. Or, introduce your newest addition with adorable birth announcements.

it's a girl

Whether you choose pink patterned papers or blue, die cut several paper Onesies from your paper of choice and attach them to a string "clothesline" for an adorable announcement. Use adhesive foam to attach each Onesie and to elevate the grouping above the cloud-patterned paper background. Add the details— and maybe even a photo—inside. DESIGN: LISA STORMS

baby boy

Thread twine through a button and adhere it to the center of a bow for an easy accent with a big impact. The ribbon on this card accents a die-cut frame embellished with large glittered letter stickers. DESIGN: LUCY ABRAMS

we joyfully introduce

Cut, punch, and die-cut all the pieces needed to assemble your announcements; then put them together assembly-line-style to speed up the process. The layered shapes on this baby announcement are topped with a die-cut Onesie that is highlighted with a small rhinestone at the neckline. DESIGN: VALERIE SALMON

introducing ethan

Dress up a design by punching a decorative border on stamped paper and accenting it with a ribbon. A cute elephant design motif works well for a boy or a girl.

DESIGN: TRACY KYLE

it's a girl

If sweet and simple is more your style, stick with a basic design that will be especially quick to make in multiples. This card features an embossed background topped with a simple printed cardstock block and ribbons.

DESIGN: TRACY KYLE

sugar and spice

Embrace a beloved saying for introducing a new little one in your life. "Sugar and spice and everything nice" is the sentiment below a fuzzy heart on this simply stated card that could serve as an announcement or a congratulatory card. Trim the bottom of the printed strip in an inverted "V" shape and attach it to a fun patterned paper background. DESIGN: LISA STORMS

it's a girl

Let your good news peek through in this slider-style baby announcement. Use the pattern on *page 188* to cut out the shape and punch three and a half circles on the front. Carefully measure and align the words so that each will show through a circle. Arrange the rest of the information above and below the announcement so it doesn't show through the holes. DESIGN: STAFF

meet griffin

Recipients will fall in love with a breathtaking photo of your newborn baby along with the sweet design of this card. Just fill in the message with your own child's name, dotting an "i" with a punched heart. If there isn't an "i," don't worry—you can still add a heart above the printed name as an accent. Round the corners of the card and add a ribbon for the finished look.

DESIGN: JEN LESSINGER

cute as a button

A paper doily from a party supply store is an unexpected touch on this feminine card. A smattering of buttons in a variety of sizes are stitched through the centers with embroidery floss, then attached with glue dots to the doily, along with a banner with the "cute as a button" expression.

DESIGN: LISA STORMS

kelly marie smith

november 1, 2011

7 lbs, 10 oz

8:16am

Baby Kelly

Mom, Dad, and big brother, Michael,
are so glad that she's finally home.

baby kelly

Announce the latest addition to your family with this card that features a photo of your baby that's attached by tiny safety pins. Print the birth details onto white cardstock, leaving room for a small photo, then cut double-sided patterned paper as a mat, making one side long enough to fold over as a flap. Secure the pinned-on photo with adhesive foam.

DESIGN: HEATHER MELZER

ALTER THE LOOK OF PAPER

There are many ways to change paper to subdue patterns, add texture, bring in a new color, or match your theme. Try these simple suggestions to bring something new to your card making.

TOP ROW LEFT TO RIGHT: PLAIN, PAINTED, CRUMPLED, VELLUM OVERLAY
BOTTOM ROW LEFT TO RIGHT: SANDED, TEA-STAINED, INKED, TEXTURE-STAMPED

congratulations on your adoption

congratulations on your adoption

Give a cute die cut an extra boost with the help of dimensional accents. This little giraffe takes on the role of child's pull toy with the help of a pair of wooden buttons for "rolling" and a long string for "tugging." Trim the bottom edge of the patterned paper background with scallop-edge scissors and add a printed banner with a congratulatory message. DESIGN: LISA STORMS

special delivery

Share the exciting news of your new baby with this postage-stamp-inspired birth announcement. Pick out your favorite newborn photo and mount it onto a white cardstock rectangle trimmed with a postage-stamp-like decorative edge. Print the information on the lower half of a piece of contrasting cardstock, leaving space for a banner printed with the words "Special Delivery" and accented with small buttons. DESIGN: LISA STORMS

Special Delivery

Jack and Maureen Ward
are proud to announce

Evan Thomas

March 2, 2011 at 2:59 pm
9 pounds 3 ounces and 19 inches

welcome handsome boy

Tiny and cute just like a brand-new baby boy describes the sweet-as-can-be striped bow tie on this card. Fashioned from striped ribbon, this little accent is sure to boost the cute factor. Spell out the announcement using alternating colors of letter stickers to match the colors used in the bow tie. DESIGN: LISA STORMS

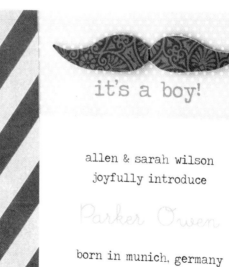

it's a boy

Never mind that he doesn't have facial hair quite yet— the adoption of a little boy is definitely something to celebrate. Announce the good news with this trendy computer-printed card featuring a hand-cut mustache and barber-shop-pole-inspired border. DESIGN: LISA STORMS

it's a boy!

allen & sarah wilson
joyfully introduce

Parker Owen

born in munich, germany
on january 22, 2011

welcomed home
on february 17, 2011

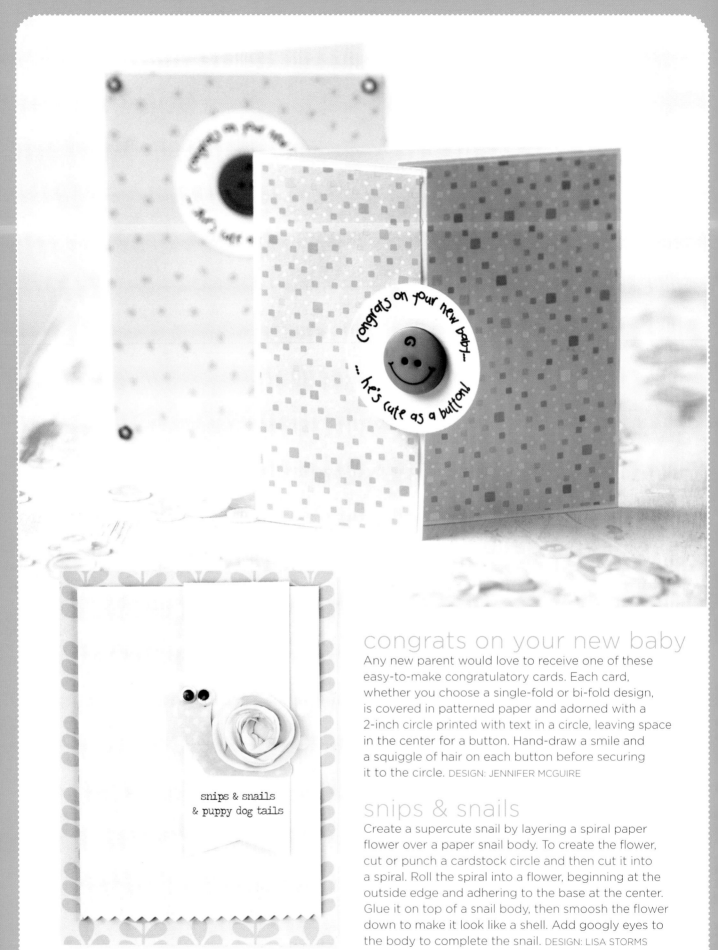

congrats on your new baby

Any new parent would love to receive one of these easy-to-make congratulatory cards. Each card, whether you choose a single-fold or bi-fold design, is covered in patterned paper and adorned with a 2-inch circle printed with text in a circle, leaving space in the center for a button. Hand-draw a smile and a squiggle of hair on each button before securing it to the circle. DESIGN: JENNIFER MCGUIRE

snips & snails

Create a supercute snail by layering a spiral paper flower over a paper snail body. To create the flower, cut or punch a cardstock circle and then cut it into a spiral. Roll the spiral into a flower, beginning at the outside edge and adhering to the base at the center. Glue it on top of a snail body, then smoosh the flower down to make it look like a shell. Add googly eyes to the body to complete the snail. DESIGN: LISA STORMS

snips & snails & puppy dog tails

congrats on your new baby— ... he's cute as a button!

halloween

Turn up the spook factor with a greeting for your favorite trick-or-treater. These merry, not scary, cards and invites come alive with spiderwebs, friendly ghosts and goblins, and other Halloween characters and icons.

trick or treat

Halloween-themed word-print paper dominates the background of this Halloween card. Although the background is busy, it works well with the greeting, which is a single phrase cut from the same word-print paper, but in black and matted with black cardstock. A striped border separated by a strip of solid cardstock provides visual relief between the patterned papers, and a striking chipboard house with vellum accent completes the design. DESIGN: MELISSA INMAN

happy halloween

Stamping is a great way to elevate an already nice card element into an outstanding one. The lined die-cut frame used as this card's central element looked a little barren, so instead of writing a message on it, stamped stars enliven the space. To avoid stamping on the border, use sticky notes to block areas where you don't want ink. DESIGN: MELISSA INMAN

come hang with us

Use a child's spiral-drawing toy to draw a silvery spiral web on dark cardstock for the front of this card. Trim the drawn shape into a rectangle, mount it onto patterned papers, and draw a straight line from the center of the spiral to the bottom of the rectangle. Adhere a plastic spider to the bottom of the line and add a greeting cut into small strips that are inked along the edges. DESIGN: LISA STORMS

You are invited to a frightfully fun

Halloween Party!

Logan's House
Saturday, October 30th
5:00 – 7:00 p.m.

Be sure to wear your costume!

frightfully fun halloween party

Put a Halloween spin on a simple invitation by turning a ribbon tie into a frightfully fun bat. To make the bat, feed wide black ribbon from the front through two holes punched through the vellum and patterned paper layers, cross the ribbon in the back, and bring the ends back through opposite holes toward the front. Trim the ribbon ends at an angle and add googly eyes to transform the ribbon into a flapping personality. DESIGN: LISA STORMS

happy halloween

Create the look of patterned paper by applying a large rub-on to a plain cardstock background. This large-scale spiderweb looks perfect on black cardstock, and is accented with a few glitter-coated brads. A sticker title matches the sophistication of the metallic-sheen rub-on.

DESIGN: MARIA CHARBONNEAUX

APPLY A RUB-ON STEP-BY-STEP

Embellish your cards with rub-on words and motifs for instant flair.

① Gather your materials: cardstock, sheet of rub-ons, scissors, applicator.

② Cut out the image you want to use. (If you transfer your rub-on from the full sheet, you run the risk of transferring pieces from around your image.) Keep the backing with the image so you don't accidentally transfer it before you're ready.

③ Discard the backing sheet and position the image. Use the applicator to rub the entire image. Peel away the plastic covering. If you find that not all of the image has transferred, carefully place the covering back down and keep rubbing.

bugs and hisses

Before you're tempted to pop that leftover piece of bubble wrap, put it to use as a stamp to make this simple, whimsical card. Brush purple paint onto the raised areas of a small piece of bubble wrap, leaving one bubble unpainted. Use a small paintbrush to paint the last bubble black, then turn the bubble wrap over and stamp it onto a piece of light purple card stock. When the paint is dry, trim the card stock into a small rectangle. Finish it with a hand-drawn spider and two googly eyes.
DESIGN: LISA STORMS

you're invited

A ribbon-wrapped rectangle makes for an irresistible mummy on the front of this fun Halloween invitation. To make the mummy, glue two googly eyes to the top half of a white cardstock rectangle, then wrap white ribbon around the cardstock so the eyes peek through a gap. Distress the edges of the rectangle and a separate piece of white ribbon with light brown ink, and hand write the party specifics onto the ribbon piece. Attach the ribbon end to the back of the mummy before attaching the mummy to the orange card base. DESIGN: LISA STORMS

smell my feet

The ghost on the front of this card is actually a child's footprint in disguise! Paint the bottom of a young child's foot with white paint, then help her press the paint onto a piece of blue cardstock, being careful to not smear the print; let dry. Draw eyes and a mouth onto the print using a black marker. DESIGN: LISA STORMS

boo

Share your Halloween memories on a photo card spun with webbed detail. Mat your favorite snapshot onto black cardstock trimmed with decorative-edge scissors, then wrap white or silver thread around the corners, taping the ends to the back. Attach the matted photo to a folded piece of cardstock, and spell out "Boo" beneath the photo with a letter sticker and two googly eyes. DESIGN: LISA STORMS

i vant to...

You can craft this cute Halloween party invite using paper scraps. To make Dracula, cut a circle from both black and light blue cardstock, then trim the black circle to mimic Dracula's hair; attach the hair to the top of the blue circle. Create the facial features with googly eyes and a small punched light blue circle for the nose; hand-draw the smile and add small white triangles for the fangs. This card was sized to fit inside a business-size envelope. DESIGN: LISA STORMS

Come have a
howling good time!
Halloween Party
Ally's House
Saturday, October 30th
5:30 – 7:30 p.m.

Be sure to wear
your costume!

howling
good time

Don't be scared off by homemade Halloween invitations.
This super-easy card uses cotton balls and a large cardstock
circle to create an eerie full moon scene. Print your party details
onto gold cardstock and use a large circle template or circle
cutter to cut out the full moon shape. Adhere pulled-apart
cotton balls to the card for the clouds. DESIGN: LISA STORMS

happy halloween

Give a witch hat elegant style by using paper with foiled flourishes for the hat and textured cardstock for the brim. The effect is subtle, but it creates realistic depth on a one-dimensional paper piecing. Use the pattern on *page 186* to cut out the pieces.

DESIGN: STAFF

✳ To make the witch hat accent, rough up the edges of an orange cardstock circle with a distressing tool to give it dimension. Top the circle with a brad and gem, and add it to the piecing.

SET AN EYELET STEP-BY-STEP
Use eyelets to add interest to your cards.

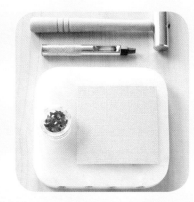

① Gather your materials: hammer, anywhere eyelet setting tool, eyelets, work mat, paper.

spooky!

On this Halloween card, strips of patterned paper are accented with a felt star and a flourish. The bottom of the card has a scalloped border, which you can either cut yourself using decorative-edge scissors or choose from a wide selection of precut trims that are available at crafts stores. The star is punctuated with an eyelet through its center. To learn how to set an eyelet, see *below*. DESIGN: TERESA LAURENZO

② Make a hole compatible with the size of the eyelet in the desired location. Insert the eyelet so the decorative side shows on the front of your design, then turn over the paper.

③ Place the eyelet setter on top of the back of the eyelet, and hammer several times. Don't hammer too firmly—you'll crush the decorative front. Lift the eyelet setter to make sure the eyelet is set firmly against the paper.

④ Turn the paper over to see the decorative eyelet. If the eyelet looks distorted, you probably hammered too firmly. Practice a few times to perfect the technique.

pumpkin

This simple jack-o'-lantern card leaves room for all kinds of possibilities and makes a great project for both adults and kids. Use a rounded square cardstock base and simply embellish it with your own cutouts or punched shapes for the face. DESIGN: LISA STORMS

join us

Even the kids can help put their stamp on this family-friendly invite. Trim a piece of black cardstock to the desired card size with rounded corners, and attach it to a slightly larger colored cardstock card base with rounded corners. Brush white paint onto your kids' fingertips, then press their fingertips onto the black cardstock in sets of two; let dry. Draw on pupils with a black marker. Finish the card with a letter-sticker greeting.

DESIGN: LISA STORMS

monster bash

Invite all the ghosts and ghouls in the neighborhood to your Halloween gathering with this monstrously easy invite. Cut out a rounded rectangle from polka-dot-patterned paper using pinking shears for the creature's body, leaving one edge straight. Add a large wiggly eye to the top of the body, and add a smaller googly eye for the "o" in the "monster bash" greeting. DESIGN: LISA STORMS

bat

Set the tone for a fun Halloween with a batty card that opens to reveal a message inside. Both wings fold to function as card flaps and are sprayed with black glitter for a shimmering look. White thread is strung through holes poked in the bottom of each wing and secured at the top with knots. The pattern is on *page 187*.
DESIGN: CATHY BLACKSTONE

MORE HALLOWEEN EMBELLISHMENTS

Embellish your Halloween cards with these piecings and include mismatched buttons and googly eyes to give them quirky character. The patterns are on *pages 186 and 189*.

skull

Boost the spook factor of your Halloween card with a glittery skull sticker strategically positioned to show off the design of tone-on-tone paper. Instead of adding a message to the front, save it for the inside of the card instead. DESIGN: MELISSA INMAN

happy halloween

Short on time but still want to send a handcrafted card? Pair a tone-on-tone patterned paper with a Halloween-themed dimensional sticker. Look for stickers with epoxy or glitter finishes for an even bigger impact. DESIGN: MELISSA INMAN

boo!

When spelling out a card's greeting, it's fun to look for interesting ways to illustrate letters instead of the usual alphabet variety. This Halloween card spells out the word "Boo" with pumpkin-shaped chipboard pieces in place of the "o"s. A hand-stitched border frames the word, giving it folk-art flair. DESIGN: ANN BLEVINS

happy halloween

Halloween papers are brimming with playful patterns and colorful dots and stripes. Trim a few strips from your favorites and use them to create a staggered background behind a Halloween-themed chipboard frame. If you don't have a chipboard frame, make your own by cutting a window from a piece of plain chipboard or heavy cardstock and covering the frame with patterned paper and adding pen details. DESIGN: MELISSA INMAN

winter holidays

Whether you celebrate Christmas or Hanukkah or are just looking for general winter-themed cards, you'll find holiday greetings to suit every taste. Plus, you can use your supplies to make great gift-card holders, tags, and wraps.

celebrate the season

Construct your own winter wonderland by making a fun, interactive snow globe from cardstock and a plastic sheet protector using the patterns on *page 189*. The snowman is embellished with buttons and pen and is sandwiched between two circles cut from a plastic sheet protector and a ripped white cardstock circle for the snowy interior. Machine-stitching holds the pieces together. When stitching, be sure to leave a small opening at the bottom for inserting glitter flakes before closing the hole. Use crafting metal and the base pattern for the bottom of the globe, embossing it as desired.

DESIGN: HELEN NAYLOR

winter

These cheery snowmen bear seasonal greetings sure to make anyone smile. Use the patterns on *page 188* to cut out the snowmen, then assemble and embellish each with pen. After adhering the snowmen to the card front, stitch the arms with tan thread and attach an acrylic letter to each snowman's belly to spell out your message.

DESIGN: HELEN NAYLOR

let it snow

Let snowy-themed patterned paper shine in a grid of four squares. For the border, gather a strip of cardstock rather than ribbon. Cut a strip twice as wide as your card, then run the barrel of the pen over it as though you're curling a ribbon. This will make it easier to shape. Run a strip of double-sided tape along one side, then create four loops as you attach it to the card. Add gems for a little sparkle.

DESIGN: VICKI BOUTIN

love

There's no need to shy from using large-scale patterned papers on a card. A beautiful traditional pattern makes a nice background for a dimensional reindeer sticker, and the layers of solid tan and white cardstock positioned between them helps the sticker pop off the background. DESIGN: MELISSA INMAN

joy

If sophisticated is the style you're looking for, try using just two neutral shades for a wintry greeting and add a bit of metallic for some shine. This oblong card is constructed with tan tone-on-tone cardstock and is backed with metallic gold cardstock for a shimmery background. A dimensional white reindeer sticker and a "Joy" message placed near the bottom of the card give it a clean look.

DESIGN: MELISSA INMAN

joy to the world

Stamp an empty frame onto plain cardstock and add
a rub-on phrase to make an elegant Christmas card design.
A narrow band of patterned paper wrapped around the sides
of the card helps to visually ground the frame and connect
it to the rest of the card design. DESIGN: MELISSA INMAN

noel

Get creative with your text by replacing the
"o" in your greeting with a dangling ornament
charm to emphasize the holiday theme.
Trim ribbon scraps to create a mitered frame
around the greeting.

warm holiday wishes and happy holidays

If you're struggling with trying to find a pleasing patterned paper and sticker combination for your Christmas cards, try using a precoordinated set. Mat the stickers with solid or subtly patterned papers to help them stand out against a busy patterned paper background.

DESIGN: MELISSA INMAN

trees

You can whip up these cards by the dozens by snipping scraps of patterned paper and attaching them to a kraft cardstock bakground—or faster yet, attach them to premade cardstock bases. The primtive trees are topped with punched stars. If using purchased card bases, look for ones with embossed borders to frame the design.

DESIGN: MELISSA INMAN

merry christmas

Two shades of green cardstock add depth to this card's funky tree. Each branch cutout is embellished with a swirly lines stamp and was heat-embossed with gold powder to create the tree's garland. Dots of metallic blue paint were dabbed on to create the ornaments. To create your own tree, use the pattern on *page 190*. DESIGN: ERIKIA GHUMM

a merry little christmas

Printed digital elements form the basis for this hybrid card. The tags are printed on photo paper, cut out, and added to the card with traditional scrapbooking supplies. Save time and money by printing multiple elements on an 8½×11-inch sheet.

DESIGN: LESLIE LIGHTFOOT

happy holidays

Glitter-covered chipboard letters spell out a holiday greeting on the front of this card. A dimensional Christmas tree sticker that extends beyond the card's top edge completes the look in a snap. DESIGN: MELISSA INMAN

fa la la la

Make a brilliant but inexpensive star by sprinkling confetti and glitter on a glue-covered cardstock shape, then attach a tinsel crafts stem. Cut costs further by swapping home-printed letters for sticker letters. DESIGN: JOHANNA PETERSON

'tis the season

When you need cards by the dozens, going digital can't be
beat. Use your word-processing program or image-editing
software and a holiday dingbat font to design the greeting.
Then create colored boxes and repeat a Christmas tree pattern
down the side to make these quick-and-easy holiday cards.
DESIGN: JEN LESSINGER

noel

It's amazing what just a
couple of punches can do
for a card design. The
greeting itself was printed
onto four different cardstock
colors, then each letter was
punched out with a large
square punch and mounted
onto the card front using
adhesive foam. The jagged
edge at the bottom of the
card front was cut with a
crafts knife, then embellished
with small punched squares
to create diamond-shaped
accent pieces. DESIGN:
GABRIELLA HUNTER

sending cheerful holiday wishes

cheerful holiday wishes

Turn wallet-size photos into giant postage stamps with decorative-edge scissors, then attach them with adhesive foam for extra oomph. Print or hand write your sentiment for an inexpensive alternative for stamps, rub-ons, or stickers. DESIGN: LISA STORMS

Spruce up gift tags with your own holiday-themed paper piecings. Use the holiday patterns on *pages 189-191* to make them all. DESIGNS: CATHY BLACKSTONE

1 Piece this dove from small pieces of cream patterned paper and embellish it with a googly eye and a small punched heart. Mount it on a circle cut from colored ledger paper and add a chipboard branch and a letter sticker sentiment.

2 Go retro with a tear-drop-shaped ornament embellished with hand-cut letters to spell out a holiday greeting. Mount it on an oval cardstock background for a tag that can double as a tree ornament.

3 Less than perfect circles layer together to make a whimsical ornament on this gift tag. Add a rub-on sentiment and a grouping of glitter brads to the ornament and punched motifs on the tag corners to jazz it up.

4 Top strips of green patterned paper with punched red circles to form a tree. Use the pattern to cut 25 strips in varying widths and assemble them in descending lengths.

5 Create your own snowy-looking tree by layering a white cardstock circle with white and gray punched snowflakes and circles along with a few gems. A tiny felt bird adds an unexpected touch of whimsy and color.

noel

Create a custom greeting using leftover sticker letters. This greeting uses a chipboard button for the "o" in "noel," but a real button would also do the trick. A slit in the card holds ribbon-tied tags, each featuring a photo and message about individual family members.
DESIGNS: JAMIE WATERS

holiday tags

Give your chalk a workout with gift tags that use the colorful medium in a variety of ways. Don't worry if you mess up: simply use a white eraser to remove the chalk, and try the technique again. For less mess and a design that sticks, use a spray fixative to ensure the chalk stays on your work, not on your hands. DESIGNS: TRACY KYLE

1 Brush chalk onto cardstock covered in stickers, then remove them for a negative image. Raid your stash of leftover mismatched stickers to use as masks.
2 Bring out the dimension in textured papers by rubbing chalk over them. More chalk creates a strong contrast and less adds a more subtle hint of color.
3 To make die cuts more realistic, shade with different hues of chalk.
4 Add chalkboard paint to your projects. The paint comes in many colors and can be applied to paper and other surfaces. The coolest part: chalk erases from its surface as it would on a chalkboard.
5 Find a new use for embossing templates by applying chalk over a template on cardstock for an easy background.

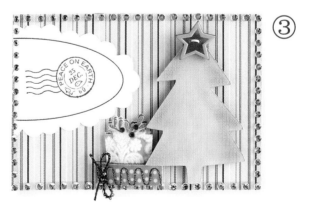

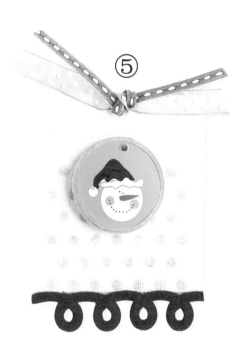

CHALK WITH A MASK STEP-BY-STEP
Use chalk to create an outline of a shape.

① Gather your materials: chalk, applicator, cardstock, sticker.

② Place your sticker on cardstock and apply chalk over it.

③ Remove the sticker to reveal an outline in chalk.

merry christmas to you!

Tags needn't be just for gifts—they make a festive addition to a card front, too. This retro snowman was stamped onto white cardstock, cut out with scalloped-edge scissors, and mounted on a red tag with a small Christmas tree sticker. The tag was then attached onto patterned cardstock using adhesive foam, then embellished with a plaid ribbon through the hole.
DESIGN: SHARON WISELY

i'll be home for christmas

Play up the lyrics of the familiar tune, "I'll Be Home for Christmas" by working a map into the background of your card. You can use patterned paper, but if you want a more custom look, print a map from the Internet or photocopy a portion of a map from an atlas. Soften the transition between different papers by tearing the edges. A traditional label maker was used to print the "Christmas" label at the corner of the card. DESIGN: NIKKI KRUEGER

happy holidays

For a low-cost card base, turn to manila folders—they're a good deal when purchased in bulk. Decorate with cardstock holly leaves and red buttons to create a festive card. To make the leaves shiny, cover green cardstock with dimensional adhesive and let it dry before cutting out the leaves and folding them lengthwise.
DESIGN: JANNA WILSON

tree gift bags

Buy basic gift bags in bulk and customize them for the holidays with paper piecings. Enlarge or reduce the pattern on a photocopier so the piecing will fit your bag. The patterns are on *page 192*.

DESIGNS: CATHY BLACKSTONE

our year in photos

A 4×6-inch photo collage accompanies a digital image of Santa Claus on this hybrid-designed card. The printed images are acccented with a chipboard star and rub-on greeting. Select sentiments from a sheet of seasonal rub-ons and hand write a message for a personal touch. DESIGN: ERIN CLARKSON

season's greetings

Don't have a good group photo? Include individual shots of family members for a simple greeting that can be printed at home or by an online printer. Going digital makes multiples a cinch—just print more copies! Or skip the printer—and the postage—and e-mail your holiday message. DESIGN: JEN LESSINGER

very merry gift cards

1 Oh So Merry To warm up your gift card, machine-stitch around three sides of a strip of stiff green felt folded in half, then adorn it with cardstock, patterned paper, and embellishments. DESIGN: LEAH FUNG

2 Gift Card Ornament Dangle your card from the tree by attaching ribbon to the back of a large chipboard snowflake and securing the gift card with repositionable adhesive. Crystals adhered to the snowflake tips, a chipboard heart accent, and a small chipboard tag round out the design. DESIGN: LEAH FUNG

3 Tree Box A die-cut box becomes a festive card carrier in a flash with a quick coat of spray ink and a few simple embellishments. DESIGN: STAFF

4 Tin Gift Card Holder Give an empty Altoids tin—which fits gift cards perfectly—a makeover by sanding and spray-painting it, then wrapping it with patterned paper and cardstock cut with decorative-edge scissors before embellishing. DESIGN: ERIKIA GHUMM

①

②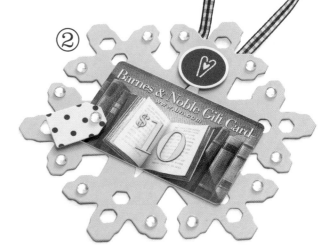

③

④

Place your sentiment behind the gift card.

happy holidays

Turn a store-bought card into a customized gift-card greeting with the addition of a jumbo photo corner stitched to the front and a printed sentiment mounted behind it. Slide a gift card into the photo corner and add chipboard snowflakes and gems to dress it and the rest of the card front up. DESIGN: LESLIE LIGHTFOOT

✻ Before you begin crafting your holiday cards, make a prototype and be sure you can find envelopes to fit it.

ho ho ho!

Stamp your background for a quick holiday card. The stamped design on this card is accented with patterned-paper strips and a die-cut star. When you have leftover bits and pieces, turn them into festive gift tags by embellishing them with die cuts, metal-rim tags, and letter stickers. DESIGN: ROBYN WERLICH

happy hanukkah

Die-cut embellishments and stamp backgrounds for a smooth assembly process. This Hanukkah card and two coordinating gift tags have stamped flourishes, borders, and star motifs topped with a die-cut Star of David and menorahs. The card also has a stamped definition and a stamped design on one of the cardstock border strips. DESIGN: NICHOL MAGOUIRK

happy hanukkah

When you want a polished look without much work, turn to a large sticker for a quick finish. This menorah sticker is mounted onto a piece of white cardstock, but rather than use a traditional Hanukkah-colored background, it pops off a background of light orange patterned paper. DESIGN: MELISSA INMAN

✳ Try these piecings for the front of your holiday cards, using the patterns on *pages 188, 189,* and *191.* To make each of the menorah candles, reduce the single candle pattern 40 percent.

FINISHING TOUCHES
Put on the gitz with embellishments that sparkle.

Dab dimensional glaze on the berries to make them gleam.

Add extra sparkle with specialty papers. The candle was constructed using mirror paper for the inner flame, glitter paper for the outer flame, and light gold metallic paper edged with iridescent glitter glue for the circular glow.

Switch papers to give the candle pattern a new look. For extra shimmer, apply gold leafing to the flames and candelabra ends.

happy hanukkah

Use the pattern on *page 188* to construct this menorah with a mix of metallic papers, cardstock, and vellum. Once your piecing is complete, position it on the card front with adhesive foam to add depth to the design. DESIGN: DEB BERGER

star of david

Simple and understated, this Hanukkah greeting features a shimmering Star of David that is framed by a cutout window in the front of the card. For an easy frame that doesn't require any measuring or cutting, simply use a silver leafing pen to outline the window. DESIGN: MELISSA INMAN

Happy Hanukkah

happy hanukkah

Ribbon scraps and glittered hearts combine forces for a colorful menorah. After adhering small pieces of ribbon, cover the bottoms with a scrap piece of cardstock, then punch nine small hearts to double as flames. DESIGN: JOHANNA PETERSON

happy hanukkah

Put your stitching skills to use by using your sewing machine to stitch the menorah on the front of a card. Lightly sketch the design using pencil, then use blue thread to stitch the lines. To create weightier lines, stitch over the lines multiple times. Not-so-perfect sewn lines add to the charm. DESIGN: CATHY BLACKSTONE

shalom

To reinforce a message of peace, cut out a dovelike bird design from a sheet of patterned paper and mount it onto a card front. If you can't find patterned paper with the right motif, search online for royalty-free clip art images and print them out. DESIGN: MELISSA INMAN

menorah

A small charm can easily get lost on a card design. To help it have more presence, mat it with a contrasting piece of cardstock before mounting it onto the card. The menorah charm onto this greeting was attached to cardstock printed with a circular pattern containing the words "Happy Hanukkah." The motif was then punched out with a large circle punch and matted on a contrasting, slightly larger cardstock circle.

DESIGN: HELEN NAYLOR

happy hanukkah

Create a clever Star of David motif using punched circles, eyelets, and string. Each circle is positioned as a point on the star and is attached to the card front with an eyelet through its center. Metallic string wound around the eyelets creates the shape that frames the "Happy Hanukkah" greeting in the center.

DESIGN: CATHY BLACKSTONE

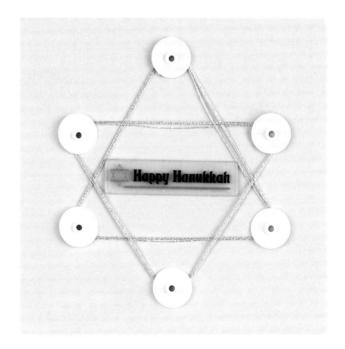

shalom

If contemporary is more your style, try this striking card design. Cut strips from both dark and light blue vellum papers (uneven cuts add to the interesting composition) and lay them across the front of a white cardstock card. Experiment by layering lighter colors over darker ones. Then punch three dark blue vellum stars and attach them on top of the stripes in a staggered arrangement, and spell out the word "shalom" using brads topped with round letter stickers.

DESIGN: ANITA MATEJKA

happy hanukkah

Blue-and-white vellum with a subtle pattern makes a wonderful soft background for a Hanukkah card. Topped with a ready-made Hanukkah sentiment sticker and a dangling punched Star of David, it's an easy custom card to make in a flash. If you can't find the right embellishment to feature, make your own with your word-processing program, a few fun fonts, and your home printer.

DESIGN: MELISSA INMAN

patterns

Find patterns for select paper-piecings and cards among these pages. Resize the patterns as needed to fit your own cards.

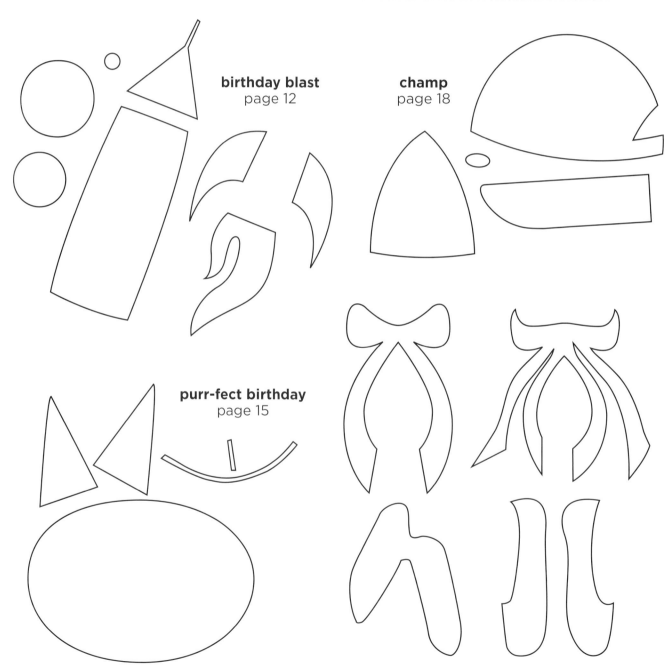

birthday blast
page 12

champ
page 18

purr-fect birthday
page 15

ballet shoes piecing
page 19

**baseball
mitt piecing**
page 19

hello friend
page 29

kite piecing
page 19

ladybug piecing
page 31

butterfly piecing
page 31

flower piecing
page 31

woodsy mushroom
page 35

april showers
page 30

thanks a latte
page 34

please join us
page 99

deer piecings
page 39

welcome home
page 38

hugs
page 53

cupcake piecing
page 58

owl in tree piecing
page 39

bee mine
page 58

hoo loves you?
page 51

you're sweet
page 68

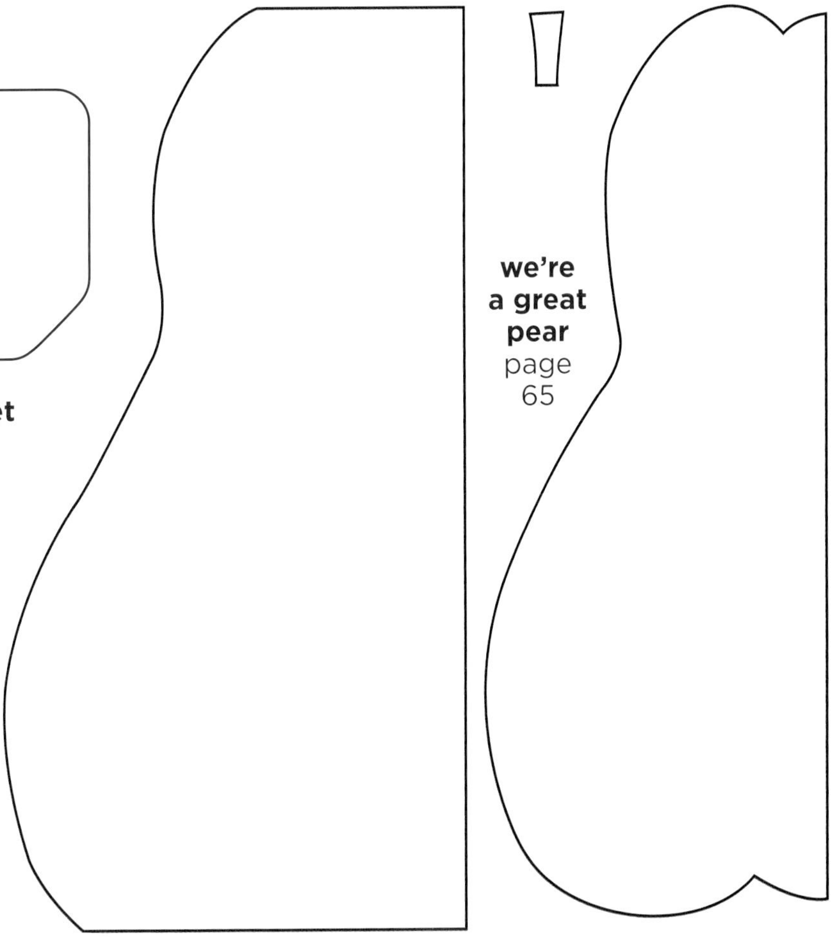

**we're
a great
pear**
page
65

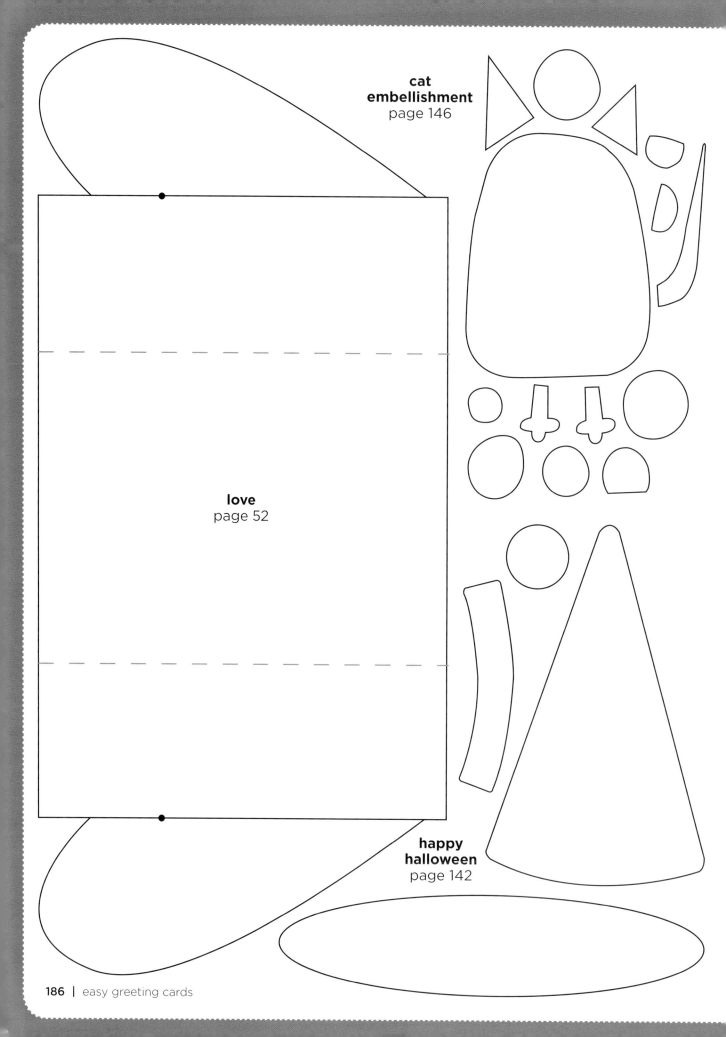

cat
embellishment
page 146

love
page 52

happy
halloween
page 142

bunny
page 72

bat
page 146

happy mother's day
page 82

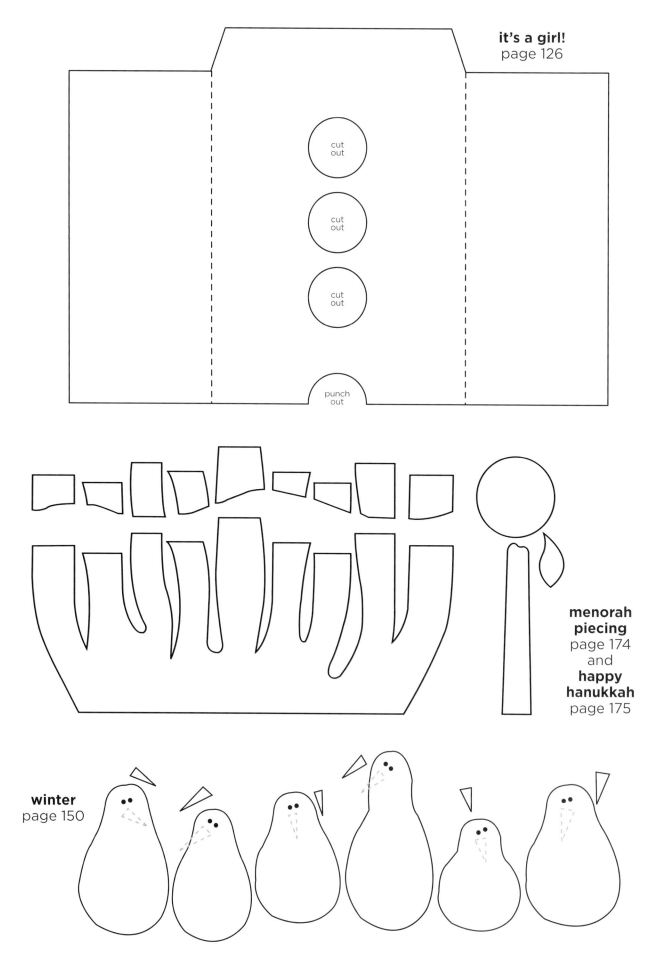

it's a girl!
page 126

cut out

cut out

cut out

punch out

menorah piecing
page 174
and
happy hanukkah
page 175

winter
page 150

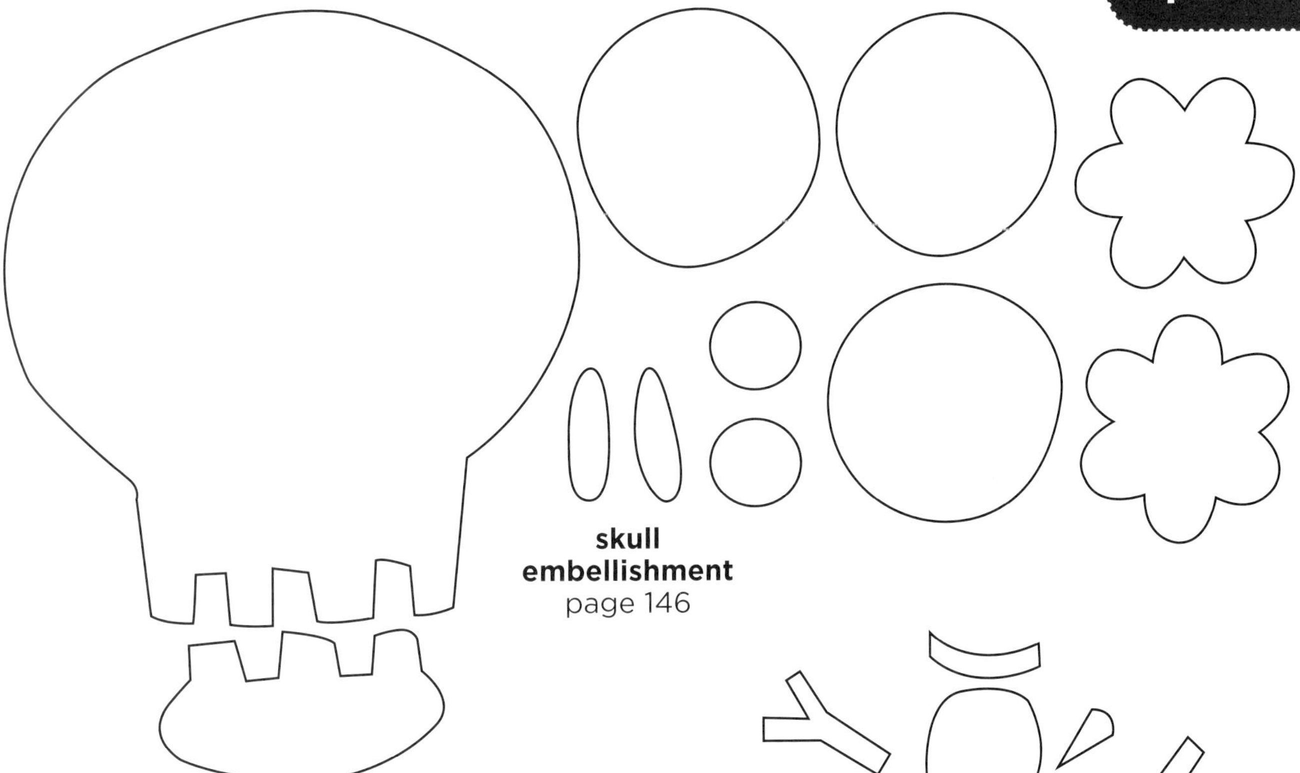

**skull
embellishment**
page 146

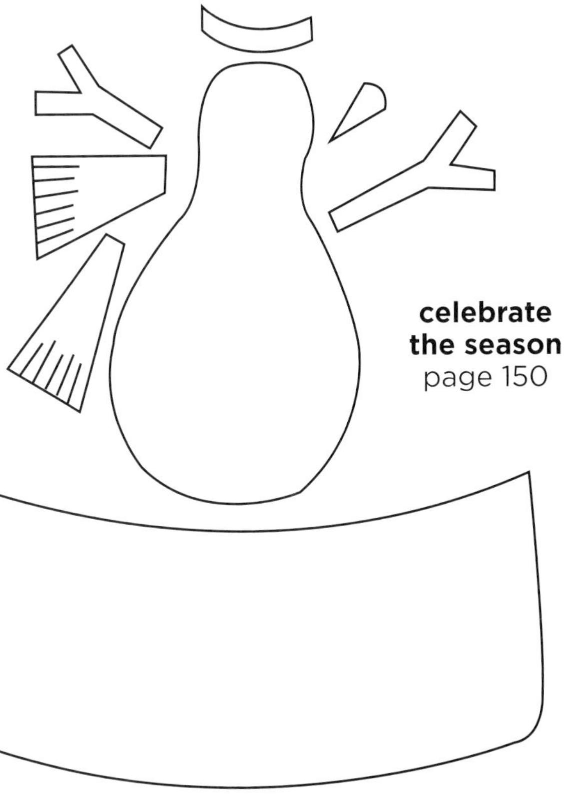

**celebrate
the season**
page 150

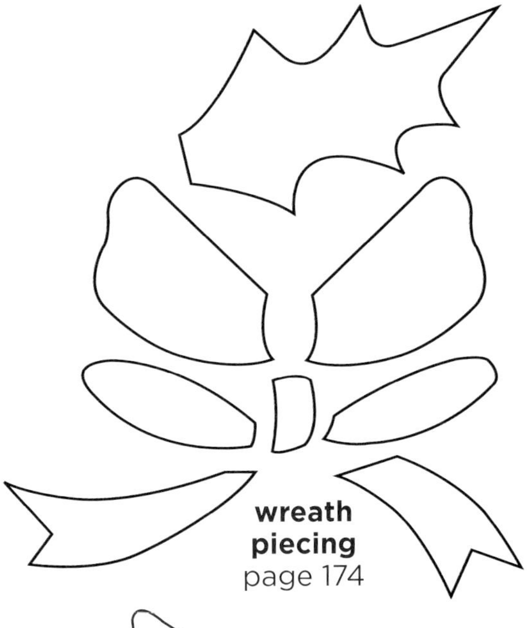

**wreath
piecing**
page 174

dove tag
page 163

merry christmas
page 157

round ornament tag
page 163

strip tree tag
page 163

candle piecing
page 174

joy tear-drop ornament tag
page 163

round-top tree tag
page 163

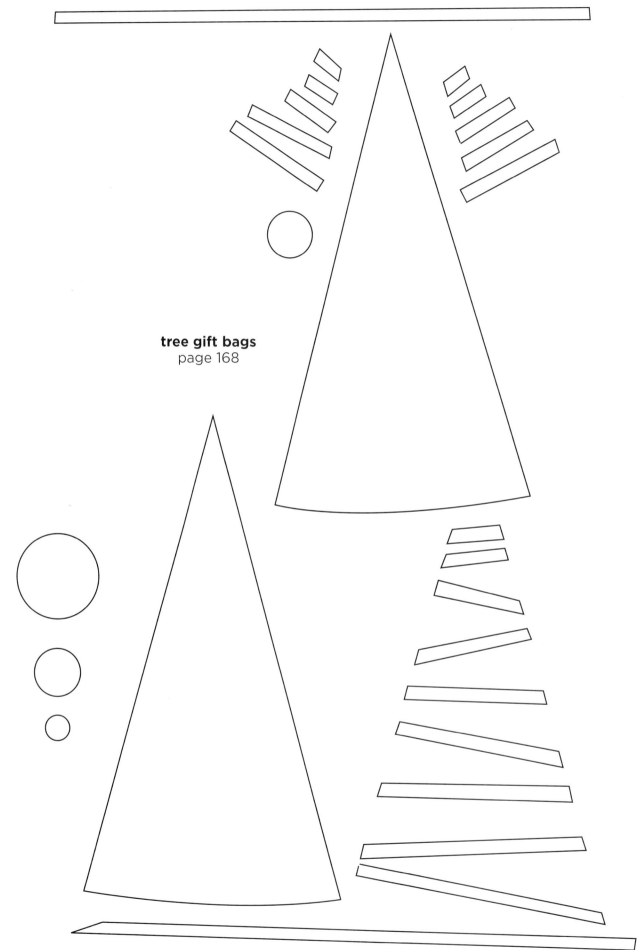

tree gift bags
page 168